LONGMAN
Photo Dictionary

3RD EDITION

ACKNOWLEDGEMENTS

Editorial Director
Michael Mayor

Publishing Manager
Laurence Delacroix

Project Editor
Nicky Thompson

Design
Matthew Dickin
Ken Vail Graphic Design

Picture Editor
Sarah Purtill

Photography
Hart McLeod
Trevor Clifford

Production
Keeley Everitt

Audio Manager
Sarah Woollard

Conversation activities & exercises
Vessela Gasper

Pronunciation Editor
Dinah Jackson

The publishers would like to thank the teachers who took part in the research for this new edition:

Lisa Anton, Jayne Bullock, Pamela Bullock, Wendy Castleton,
Helen Diver, Hailu Embaye, Ros Leather, Tom Lloyd, Siobhan Markwell,
Tracie Morrison, Marinela Papleka, Florence Pinard, Mark Pope,
Alison Robinson, Delia Rodriguez, Lesley Slater, Amanda Stewart,
Jo Thorp, Mustafa Uruncuoglu, Emily Vivas, Atin Wickham

Pearson Education Limited
Edinburgh Gate
Harlow
Essex CM20 2JE
England
and Associated Companies throughout the world

Visit our website: www.pearsonELT.com/dictionaries

First published 2001
Second edition 2006
Third edition 2010
20 19 18 17
IMP 12 11 10 9 8

ISBN: 978-1-4082-6195-8 (paper + audio CDs)

British Library Cataloguing-in-Publication Data
A catalogue record for this book is available from the British Library.

Set in Frutiger by Ken Vail Graphic Design, Cambridge
Printed in China
SWTC/08

The new *Longman Photo Dictionary* is a vocabulary resource book for learners of English from beginner's level. It contains more than 3,500 words covering over 95 different topics – all clearly introduced through hundreds of colour photographs. Words are grouped together and presented either contextually: everyday life vocabulary relating to housing and food are grouped in sections such as *The bathroom, The kitchen, At the supermarket, Vegetables* and so on, or thematically: words relating to specific topics are grouped in sections such as *Computers, Jobs, Sports* and *Animals*.

The *Longman Photo Dictionary* can be used by beginners for learning new vocabulary as well as by more advanced students as a quick reference. In the classroom it will help students to learn new words in context or build up vocabulary relating to a particular lesson, to practise pronunciation, alphabetisation and grouping words by topics, or it can be used at home for practical help with everyday vocabulary.

Pick and choose

Each section is self-contained and can be used at any time, in random order and adapted to any teaching situation: to consolidate known vocabulary, to learn new words, to practise oral conversation or as a practical reference guide to help in everyday life.

Exercises and grammar

Conversation practice
Short conversation activities on each page cover basic grammar points (progressive form, prepositions, basic structures, etc) and stimulate communication, helping students to express themselves, showing them how to describe things, people and situations or talk about personal opinions.

Exercises
Controlled exercises at the back offer further written practice to recycle the words presented in the book. These will help students memorise new vocabulary in an enjoyable way, with puzzles, matching activities, categorising, etc, and help them use words in full sentences.

Word list with pronunciation

The 3,500 words are listed in alphabetical order with phonetic pronunciations. If students come across a word they don't know, they can find a photo quickly, understand what it means immediately and check the correct pronunciation.

Audio CDs

Students can also listen to all the words pronounced on the audio CDs.

CONTENTS

CONTENTS

1 name
2 surname / family name
3 first name
4 initials
5 title
6 age
7 sex
8 marital status
9 date of birth
10 village, town or city of birth
11 nationality
12 National Insurance number
13 country of birth
14 next of kin
15 address
16 postcode
17 daytime telephone number
18 mobile phone number
19 e-mail address

Application Form

Please complete all of the items on the form to the best of your knowledge. Use blue or black ink only.

① Surname ② SMITH
First name JOHN ③   Initials JS ④
Title MR ⑤ Age 25 ⑥ Sex Male ✓ ⑦ Female ☐ (please tick)
⑧ Marital status single ✓ married ☐ divorced ☐ widow/widower ☐ (please tick)
Date of birth day 07 month MAY year 1985 ⑨   Village, town or city of birth BRISTOL ⑩
Nationality BRITISH ⑪
National Insurance number ⑫
Country of birth UNITED KINGDOM ⑬
⑭ Next of kin
Address 23 SOUTHFIELD ROAD
PURBEY ⑮
WESTSHIRE   Postcode PU23 4HJ ⑯
Daytime telephone number 0560 152439 ⑰   Mobile phone number ⑱
E-mail address jsmith@internetsp.com ⑲

20 single
21 married
22 divorced
23 widow / widower
24 birth certificate
25 passport
26 driving licence
27 ID (identity) card
28 child
29 baby
30 toddler
31 teenager
32 adult
33 elderly (old)
34 girl
35 boy
36 man
37 woman
38 couple

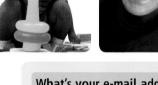

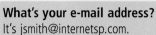

What's your e-mail address?
It's jsmith@internetsp.com.

Do you have a driving licence?
Yes, I do. / No, I don't.

A What's your ....?
B It's ....

A Do you have a / an ....?
B ....

Questions for discussion
1 Give the personal data of a famous person.
2 When was the last time you completed an application form? What information did you have to provide?

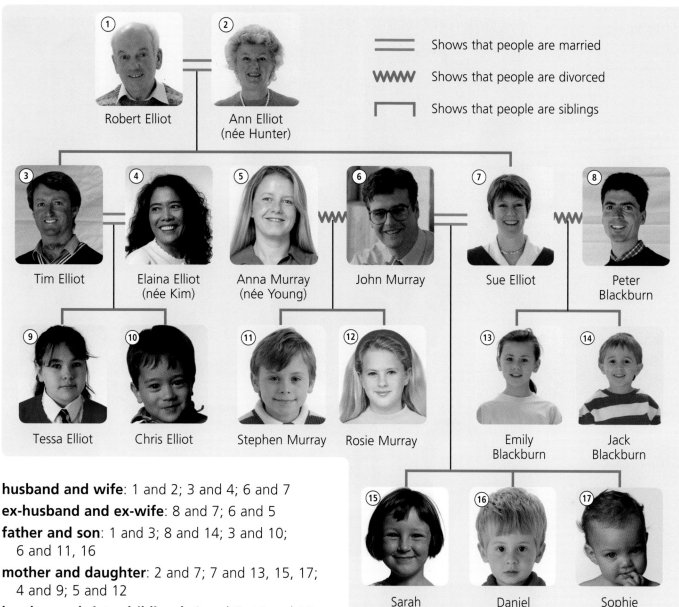

Shows that people are married

Shows that people are divorced

Shows that people are siblings

1 Robert Elliot
2 Ann Elliot (née Hunter)
3 Tim Elliot
4 Elaina Elliot (née Kim)
5 Anna Murray (née Young)
6 John Murray
7 Sue Elliot
8 Peter Blackburn
9 Tessa Elliot
10 Chris Elliot
11 Stephen Murray
12 Rosie Murray
13 Emily Blackburn
14 Jack Blackburn
15 Sarah Elliot-Murray
16 Daniel Elliot-Murray
17 Sophie Elliot-Murray

husband and wife: 1 and 2; 3 and 4; 6 and 7

ex-husband and ex-wife: 8 and 7; 6 and 5

father and son: 1 and 3; 8 and 14; 3 and 10; 6 and 11, 16

mother and daughter: 2 and 7; 7 and 13, 15, 17; 4 and 9; 5 and 12

brother and sister (siblings): 3 and 7; 14 and 13; 10 and 9; 16 and 15, 17; 11 and 12

sisters-in-law: 7 and 4   **brothers-in-law**: 3 and 6

father-in-law and son-in-law: 1 and 6

mother-in-law and daughter-in-law: 2 and 4

parent(s) and child(ren): 1, 2 and 3, 7; 7, 8 and 13, 14; 3, 4 and 9, 10; 5, 6 and 11, 12; 6, 7 and 15, 16, 17

grandparents and grandchildren: 1, 2 and 9, 10, 13, 14, 15, 16, 17

grandfather and grandson: 1 and 10, 14, 16

grandmother and granddaughter: 2 and 9, 13, 15, 17

uncle and nephew: 3 and 14, 16

aunt and niece: 4 and 13, 15, 17; 7 and 9

cousins: 13, 14 and 9, 10

single parent: 5

remarried: 6 and 7

stepfather and stepdaughter: 6 and 13

stepmother and stepson: 7 and 11

stepbrother and stepsister: 14 and 12; 11 and 13

half-brother and half-sister: 11 and 15, 17; 16 and 12; 16 and 13; 14 and 15, 17

Who's she? (2)
She's Tessa's grandmother.

Who's he? (11)
He's Sophie's half-brother.

A Who's she? (7)
B She's ....

A Who's he / she?
B He's / She's ....'s ....

Questions for discussion
1 Which of these words apply to women only?
2 Which of these words apply to both men and women?
3 Draw your family tree and talk about it. Are there any relationships you cannot describe in English?

1 wake up
2 get up
3 have a shower
4 shave
5 dry yourself
6 brush your teeth
7 wash your face
8 rinse your face

9 get dressed
10 comb your hair
11 put on make-up
12 have breakfast
13 have a cup of coffee

14 go to work
15 watch (TV)
16 listen to the radio
17 read (the paper)
18 have a bath
19 brush your hair
20 go to bed
21 sleep

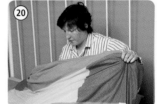

Is she waking up? (1)
Yes, she is.

Is he washing his face? (6)
No, he isn't. He's brushing his teeth.

A **Is she eating breakfast? (13)**
B ....

A **Is he / she** ....?
B Yes, he / she is. / No, he / she isn't.

Questions for discussion
1 Which of these things do you do in the morning?
2 In which order do you do them?
3 Which of these activities do you like or dislike doing?

A DETACHED HOUSE
1 porch
2 garage
3 front garden, yard *AmE*
4 drive

B TERRACED HOUSES
5 gate
6 fence

C FRONT DOOR
7 knocker
8 doorknob
9 letterbox
10 front door
11 doorbell
12 doorstep

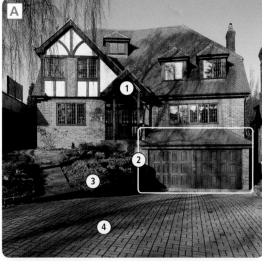

D COTTAGE
13 chimney
14 shutter
15 window

E FLATS
16 balcony

F SEMI-DETACHED HOUSE
17 TV aerial

G BUNGALOW
18 gutter   20 roof
19 satellite dish   21 drainpipe

Do you live in a cottage?
Yes, I do.

Do you live in a flat?
No, I don't. I live in a bungalow.

A **Do you live in a** ....?
B Yes, I do. / No, I don't. I live in a
....

Questions for discussion
1 Which of these places to live are common in your country? Where do you find them?
2 Describe your home.

1 tap, faucet *AmE*
2 sink
3 drawer
4 double oven
5 kitchen unit
6 cupboard
7 (cooking) pot
8 work-surface / worktop

9 hob
10 hotplate
11 (door) handle

12 dishwasher
13 bin
14 (aluminium) foil
15 clingfilm™

16 fridge / refrigerator
17 freezer
18 cafetière
19 cookery book
20 storage jar
21 spices
22 spice rack

23 washing-up liquid
24 dishcloth
25 tea towel

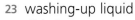

Where would you put milk?
In the fridge.

Where would you put the dirty plates?
In the dishwasher. / In the sink.

A Where would you put
.........................?
B In the ....

Questions for discussion
1 Which of these things are used for storage?
2 Which of these things are used for preparing food?
3 Which of these things are used for washing or cleaning things?

1 lid
2 wok
3 handle
4 chopping board
5 knife
6 food processor
7 microwave
8 casserole dish
9 roasting tin
10 cake tin
11 oven glove
12 baking tray
13 steamer
14 peeler
15 sieve
16 garlic press
17 toaster
18 (hand) beater /
   rotary whisk

19 blender
20 rolling pin
21 tin opener
22 ladle

23 kettle
24 measuring spoon
25 grater
26 (mixing) bowl
27 whisk
28 measuring jug
29 (electric) mixer
30 bottle opener
31 coffee maker
32 saucepan
33 frying pan

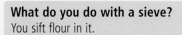

What do you do with a sieve?
You sift flour in it.

What do you do with a blender?
You mix food in it.

A What do you do with
   a ....? (24)
B You .... in / with it.

A What do you do with ....?
B You .... in / with it.

Questions for discussion
1 Which of these things do you use every day?
2 Which of these things do you need to make a cake?
3 Which of these things can you turn on / off?

1 bath
2 bath mat
3 tile
4 toilet
5 shower
6 mug
7 toothpaste
8 toothbrush
9 toothbrush holder
10 razor
11 shaving gel
12 shaving brush
13 soap

14 soap dish
15 soap dispenser
16 mirror
17 shelf
18 hot water tap
19 cold water tap
20 washbasin
21 toilet roll

22 laundry basket
23 bath towel
24 hand towel
25 towel rail
26 shower curtain
27 bathroom cabinet
28 shampoo
29 shower gel
30 conditioner
31 facecloth / flannel

Have you got a bath mat in your bathroom?
Yes, I have.

Have you got shelves in your bathroom?
No, I haven't. I've got a bathroom cabinet.

A Have you got a ....?
B Yes, I have. / No, I haven't.
    I've got ....

Questions for discussion
1 How long do you spend in the bathroom each day? Why?
2 Do you prefer having a bath or a shower? Why?

1 chest of drawers
2 drawer
3 handle
4 lamp
5 bedside table
6 wallpaper
7 (scatter) cushion
8 double bed
9 carpet
10 pillowcase
11 pillow
12 alarm clock
13 headboard
14 bedspread
15 single bed
16 blanket
17 sheet
18 (fitted) sheet
19 duvet / quilt
20 valance

21 mirror
22 dressing table
23 wardrobe
24 mattress
25 radiator

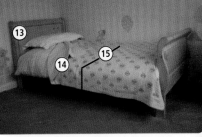

Where's the blanket?
It's on top of the sheets.

Where are the sheets?
They're underneath the duvet.

A Where are the cushions?
B They're .... the ....

A Where's / Where are the .... ?
B It's / They're underneath / on top of / next to the
....

Questions for discussion

1 What was your bedroom like when you were little?

2 What is your bedroom like now?

1 window	10 plant pot / tub	19 fireplace
2 curtain, drape *AmE*	11 armchair	20 fireguard
3 picture frame	12 cushion	21 desk
4 picture	13 coffee table	22 remote control
5 lampshade	14 flowers	23 television
6 lamp	15 vase	24 DVD player
7 bookcase	16 sofa / settee	
8 books	17 rug	
9 plant	18 mantelpiece	

Is there a fireplace in your living room?
No, there isn't.

Are there any pictures in your living room?
Yes, there are.

A **Are there any / Is there a / an**
.... **in your**
living room?

B Yes there are. / No there aren't. /
Yes, there is. / No, there isn't.

Questions for discussion
1 Which of these things can you sit on?
2 Do living rooms in your country look like this? What is different?

1 side table
2 chair
3 (dining room) table
4 candle
5 teapot
6 cake stand
7 place mat
8 salt
9 pepper
10 serving dish
11 serviette / napkin
12 serviette / napkin ring
13 tray
14 coaster

A CROCKERY

15 mug
16 jug
17 wine glass
18 cup
19 saucer
20 bowl
21 plate

B CUTLERY

22 fork
23 knife
24 dessertspoon
25 teaspoon
26 soup spoon

What do you do with a place mat?
You put your plate on it.

Where's the teaspoon?
It's to the right of the dessert spoon.

A What do you do with a ....?
B You ....

A Where's the ....?
B It's .... of the ....

Questions for discussion

1 Which of these things are used for serving food?

2 Which of these things do you use for drinking?

3 Which of these things are used for eating?

1 teat
2 (baby) bottle
3 (baby) cup
4 (box of) tissues
5 dummy
6 mobile
7 soft toy
8 teddy bear
9 cot
10 baby sling
11 baby carrier
12 sterilizer
13 potty
14 (baby) wipes
15 changing mat
16 nappy
17 car seat

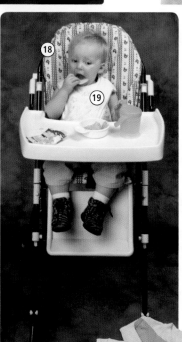

18 high chair
19 bib
20 bouncer
21 pushchair (buggy)
22 pram
23 (baby) clothes
24 intercom

Where's the baby? (11)
He's in his baby carrier.

Where's the baby? (18)
He's in his high chair.

A Where's the baby?
B He's / She's in / on his / her
....

Questions for discussion

1 Which of these things can a baby sit or lie in?

2 Which of these things are used for feeding a baby?

1 clothesline / washing line
2 peg
3 fabric conditioner
4 iron
5 socket
6 plug
7 duster
8 dustpan
9 brush
10 ironing board
11 sponge mop

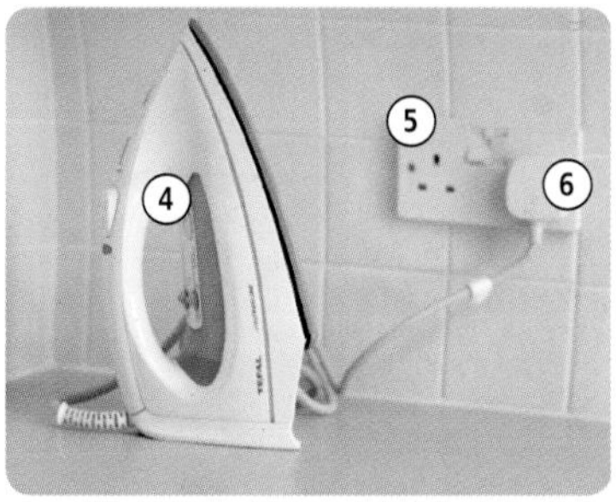

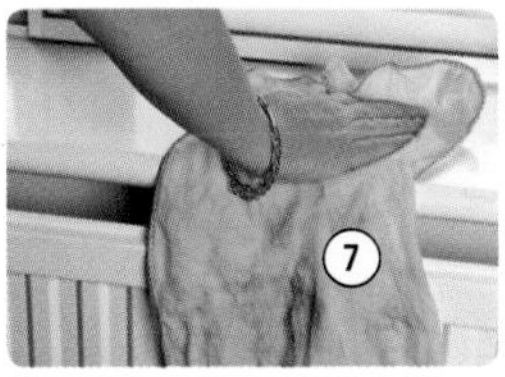

12 broom / brush
13 mop
14 bucket

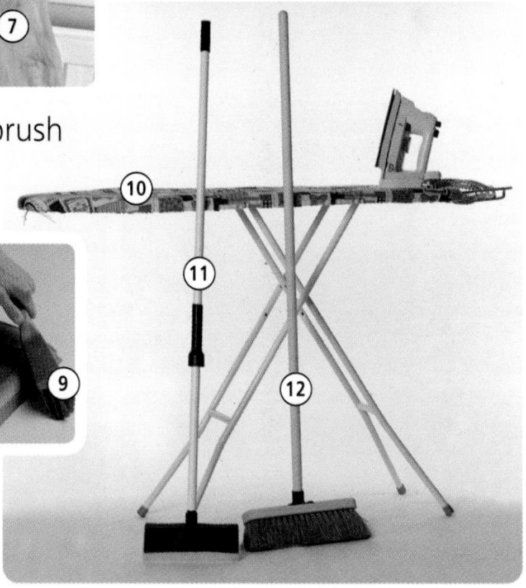

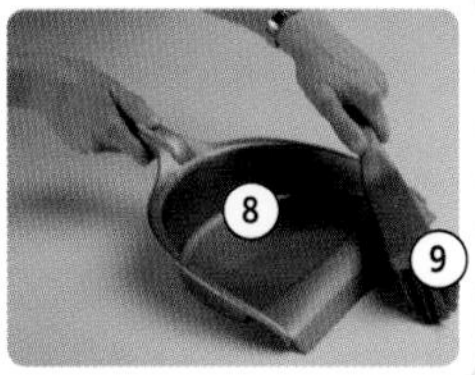

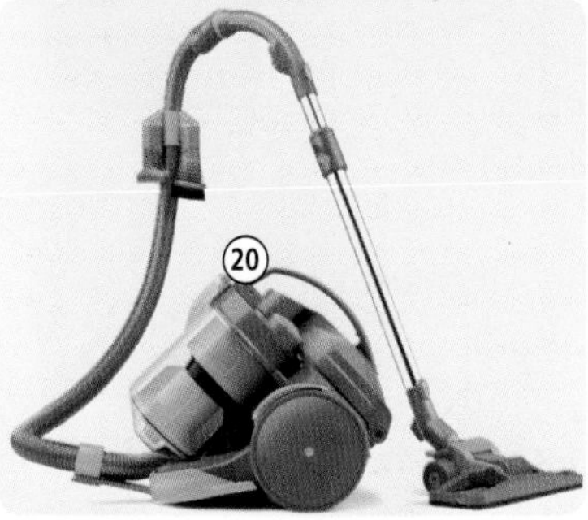

15 laundry basket
16 airer
17 washing powder
18 washing machine
19 tumble dryer
20 vacuum cleaner
21 scrubbing brush
22 coat hanger

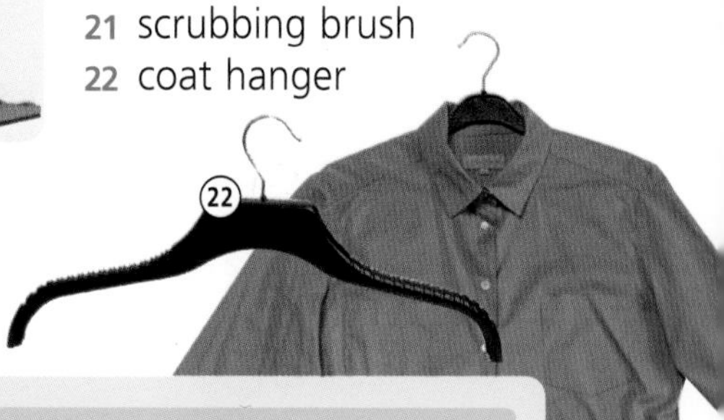

Where are the dirty clothes?
They're in the laundry basket.

What do you do with a mop?
You mop the floor.

A **Where is / are the** ....?
B It's / They're on / in / next to the ....

A **What do you do with a** ....?
B You ....

Questions for discussion
1 Who does the housework in your house?
2 Which jobs do you do?
3 How often do you use these things?

1 umbrella / parasol
2 patio
3 (patio) chair
4 (patio) table
5 flowerbed
6 lawn
7 pond
8 sun lounger
9 barbecue
10 bush
11 garden shed
12 tree
13 greenhouse
14 hedge
15 swing
16 vegetable garden
17 border

FLOWERS

18 lily
19 pansy
20 tulip
21 petunia
22 geranium
23 iris
24 chrysanthemum
25 daffodil
26 hyacinth
27 snapdragon
28 daisy
29 orchid
30 rose

Where's the table? (4)
It's on the patio, to the right of the lawn.

Where's the swing? (15)
It's on the lawn, next to the fence.

A Where's the garden shed?
B It's ....

A Where's the ....?
B It's ....

Questions for discussion
1 Do you have a garden?
2 What are your favourite flowers?
3 Describe your ideal garden.

1 lawn mower
2 watering can
3 seeds
4 seed trays
5 hedge trimmer
6 secateurs
7 shears
8 gardening gloves
9 trowel
10 slug pellets
11 potting shed
12 compost
13 rake
14 fork
15 spade
16 wheelbarrow
17 fence
18 pot / tub
19 hose / hosepipe
20 fertiliser
21 tap

22 sprinkler
23 tie up a branch
24 dig the soil
25 water the plants
26 plant flowers
27 weed the flowerbed
28 prune a shrub
29 mow the lawn

SLUG MINI-PELLETS
SHOWER PROOF
WITH SPECIAL ANIMAL REPELLENT

Van Hage
MULTI PURPOSE COMPOST

GROWMORE

I want to prune some shrubs.
You need shears or a hedge trimmer.

What do I need to plant a flower?
You need fresh soil and a trowel to dig
a hole.

A I want to ....
B You need (a) .... and / or
(a) ....

A What do I need to ....?
B You need ....

Questions for discussion

1 Which of these things do people do
in spring?

2 Do you like gardening?

3 Which of these things do you do?

1 stairs
2 ground floor
3 first floor
4 attic / loft
5 airing cupboard
6 second floor
7 ceiling
8 landing
9 floor
10 upstairs
11 downstairs
12 cellar / basement
13 utility room (see p.17)
14 kitchen (see p.10)
15 dining room (see p.15)

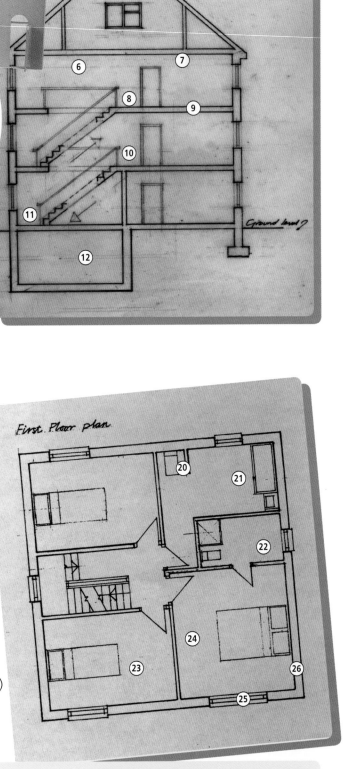

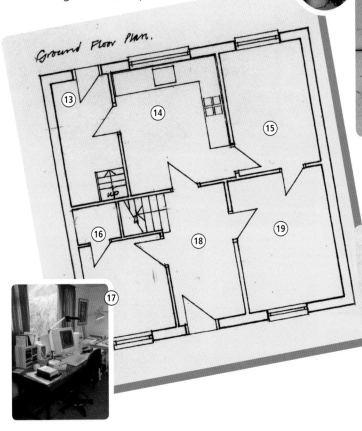

Ground Floor Plan.

First Floor plan

16 stair cupboard
17 study
18 hallway
19 living room / lounge /
   sitting room (see p.14)
20 toilet

21 bathroom (see p.12)
22 en suite shower room
23 bedroom
24 master bedroom (see p.13)
25 window
26 wall

Has your home got a kitchen / attic?	A Has your home got a ....?	**Questions for discussion**
Yes, it has. / No, it hasn't.	B Yes, it has. / No, it hasn't.	1 Which of these things are common in homes in your country?
How many bedrooms has your home got?	A **How many** .... **has your home got?**	2 Draw a floor plan of your home and describe it.
It's got two.	B It's got	

1 make the bed
2 make breakfast
3 feed the dog
4 take the children to school
5 take the bus to school

6 hoover / vacuum
7 sweep
8 wash the floor
9 dust
10 iron
11 sew
12 feed the baby
13 wash the dishes
14 load the dishwasher
15 pick up the children

16 walk the dog
17 go shopping
18 cook / make lunch / dinner
19 do the laundry
20 study
21 do homework

Did you feed the dog this morning?
Yes, I did.

Did you go shopping yesterday?
No, I didn't.

A **Did you wash the floor this morning / yesterday?**
B Yes, I did. / No, I didn't.

A **Did you .... this morning / yesterday?**
B ....

Questions for discussion

1 Which of these activities do you do every day?

2 Which activities do you like / dislike?

1 CV, résumé *AmE*
2 interview
3 application form
4 covering letter
5 telephone number
6 e-mail address
7 job board
8 job ads
9 Jobcentre Plus
10 Citizens Advice Bureau

Curriculum Vitae

Name	John Smith
Address	23 Southfield Road, Purbey, Westshire PU23 4HJ — Telephone 056... — e-mail jsmith...
Age	25
Date of birth	7 May 1985
Marital status	Single
Occupation	Sales Assistant
Education	Purbey Comprehensive School 1997-2004

Qualifications
GCSE
Mathematics B
English B
Geography A
History B
French C
Art B

A-levels
Business studies B
English C
French D

Employment
Customer services assistant – GRM Logistics
My first job involved dealing with customer queries on the phone or by post. I also helped run the customer data base and supplied information for sales managers. I had to be well organised and understand customers' needs.

Sales assistant – GRM Logistics
I directly supported the sales manager in every aspect of her work. I handled some accounts without supervision and visited these customers when necessary. Good negotiating and communication skills were essential.

Other Interests
Outside of work I am a member of the local football team and play every Saturday this also includes two nights football training during the week. I also play the drums in a band and we play clubs about three times a month.

Application for employment

Personal details

Title Mr	Date of birth 7 May 1985	Marital status S...
		Surname Smi...

First name(s) John

Address *(including postcode)*
23 Southfield Road
Purbey
Westshire
PU23 4HJ

Daytime telephone number
0763 124790

Evening telephone number
0560 152439

National Insurance number

E-mail address

Education / training

School / College / University etc attended	Qualifications gained / courses studied
Purbey Comprehensive School Beacon Road Purbey Westshire PU22 3QN	3 A-levels: Business studies, English, French
	6 GCSEs: Mathematics, English, Geography, History, French, Art
	I also hold a clean driving licence

Work history

Customer servi...
GRM Logistics,...
My first job inv...
phone or by po...
and supplied in...
organised and...

Sales assista...
GRM Logistic...
I directly supp...
work. I handle...
these custo...
communicati...

Sam's News...
I delivered n...
the counter...
on Saturday...

References

David Roo...
Beacon R...
Telephone

Mrs Julia...
7 High St...
Telephon...

23 Southfield Road, Purbey, Westshire PU23 4HJ

Telephone 0560 152439
e-mail jsmith@internetsp.com

Dear Sir/Madam,
   I am writing to apply for the position of Sales Manager advertised in The Evening Post on 24 August 2010.
   I have been working for the past two years as a sales assistant within a busy department. I believe this has given me excellent experience and the confidence to take a step forward in my career.
   As requested I enclose my full CV and application form. If there is any other information you require, please don't hesitate to contact me.

I look forward to your reply.

Yours faithfully,
John Smith
John Smith

Vacancies

Vacancy

Job title	Line manager — nights
Department	Production
Salary grade	C2
Application date	April 17
Hours	30- hour — shifts (overtime available)
Job description	The responsibility is for managing all aspects of line production on our Xexon 450 machines. Previous experience is essential. The successful candidate is likely to have worked on the Xexon line during the past two years. The ability to solve production problems at short notice is key. Night shift hours. Some weekend working.

For more information and application form

Jenny Stewart
Human Resources
Room 438
Internal tel: 2452
Intranet: j.stewart@acef.com

Vacancy

Job title	Customer Services Assistant
Department	Sales and Marketing
Salary grade	G1
Application date	April 10
Hours	24-hour minimum — negotiable
Job description	The job requires the ability to answer calls and emails from customers, provide information to them and manage a database. Full training is provided. The successful candidate will have to have a good telephone manner be polite and patient at all times. Flexible hours can be negotiated.

For more information and application form

Jenny Stewart
Human Resources
Room 438
Internal tel: 2452
Intranet: j.stewart@acef.com

jobcentreplus

citizens advice bureau
08450 505152

1 farmer
2 baker
3 mechanic
4 taxi driver
5 electrician
6 lorry driver
7 soldier
8 florist
9 window cleaner
10 carpenter

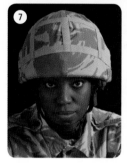

11 chef / cook
12 painter
13 waiter / waitress
14 bricklayer
15 gardener
16 greengrocer

17 plumber
18 refuse collector
19 fisherman
20 butcher
21 motorcycle courier

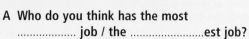

Who do you think has the most difficult / the easiest job?
A farmer. / A motorcycle courier.

A Who do you think has the most
.... job / the ....est job?
B A / An ....

Questions for discussion
Choose three jobs:
1 Do you know anyone who does these jobs?
2 What qualities do you need for these jobs?

1 vet, veterinarian *AmE*
2 nurse
3 doctor
4 pharmacist
5 fire fighter
6 scientist
7 optician
8 dentist
9 barrister / lawyer
10 judge
11 postman / postwoman
12 police officer
13 lecturer
14 teacher
15 nursery assistant

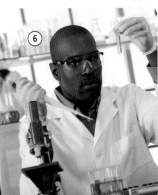

Who do you think has the most interesting / boring job?

A vet. / A teacher.

A Who do you think has the most .... job?

B ....

Questions for discussion

Choose three jobs:

1 Do you know anyone who does these jobs?

2 What qualifications do you need for these jobs?

1 journalist / reporter
2 newsreader
3 secretary / personal assistant (PA)
4 cashier
5 accountant
6 sales assistant
7 estate agent
8 shopkeeper
9 travel agent
10 bank clerk

11 receptionist
12 factory worker / blue-collar worker
13 office worker / white-collar worker
14 call centre operator
15 photographer
16 hairdresser
17 artist
18 draughtsman
19 architect
20 designer

What do reporters do?
They tell people about events.

Would you like to be a reporter?
Yes, I would. / No, I wouldn't.

A **What do** .... **do?**
B They ....

A **Would you like to be a / an** ....?
B Yes, I would. / No, I wouldn't.

Questions for discussion
Which of the jobs on pages 23–26:
1 involve hard physical work?
2 are creative?

1 train driver
2 childminder / nanny
3 cleaner
4 social worker
5 traffic warden
6 midwife
7 care worker
8 paramedic
9 network engineer
10 IT workers
11 computer programmer
12 software engineer
13 computer technician
14 technical support engineer
15 help desk operator
16 bus driver
17 plasterer
18 labourer
19 security guard

1 desk tidy
2 calendar
3 noticeboard
4 electric typewriter
5 (desk) lamp
6 computer
7 desk
8 swivel chair
9 telephone
10 in tray
11 out tray
12 files
13 paper clip holder
14 paper clips
15 desk diary
16 Sellotape™
17 correction fluid / Tipp-Ex™ *BrE*
18 Post-it™ notes

19 notepad
20 (ball point) pen / biro™
21 hole-punch
22 stapler
23 fax machine
24 franking machine
25 photocopier
26 pencil
27 elastic band / rubber band
28 rubber
29 wastepaper basket / bin
30 ring binder
31 folder
32 plastic wallet
33 highlighter

Why do people use paper clips?
They use them to fasten sheets of paper together.

A Why do people use Sellotape™?
B They use it to ....

A Why do people use ....?
B They use them / it to ....

Questions for discussion
1 Which items need electricity?
2 Which items fix things together?
3 Which items do you have in your home?

OFFICE ACTIVITIES

1 take notes
2 type
3 staple documents together
4 fill in a form
5 sign a letter
6 note appointments
7 file papers
8 filing cabinet
9 photocopy a letter
10 send a fax / fax a document
11 answer the phone
12 print a hard copy
13 greet visitors
14 offer refreshments
15 write a memo
16 send an e-mail

To: sally.harvey@google.com
Cc:
Subject: Meeting

Hi Sally,

Could you arrange a meeting for Tuesday at 10?

Thanks,
Stephen

What's she doing? (1)
She's taking notes.

What's he doing? (11)
He's answering the phone.

A **What's she doing? (7)**
B She's ....

A **What's he / she doing?**
B He's / She's ....

Questions for discussion
1 Which of these activities would a manager do?
2 Which of these activities would an assistant do?
3 Which of these activities are boring?

1 mallet
2 toolbox
3 tape measure
4 hand saw
5 hacksaw
6 power saw
7 Stanley knife™
8 hammer
9 nails
10 screwdriver
11 screws
12 nut
13 bolt
14 washer

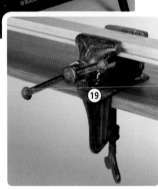

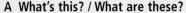

20 hatchet / axe
21 bradawl
22 square
23 power / electric drill
24 (drill) bits
25 pliers
26 (adjustable) spanner
27 file
28 wrench
29 paintbrush
30 (paint) pot
31 hook
32 (paint) tray
33 (paint) roller
34 paint

15 workbench
16 plane
17 sandpaper
18 chisel
19 vice

What's this? (8)
It's a hammer.

What are these? (11)
They're screws.

A What's this? / What are these?
B It's (a) / They're... .

Questions for discussion
Which things would you need if you wanted to:
1 make a cupboard?
2 paint your living room?

1 (assembly) line
2 machine
3 worker
4 work station
5 time clock
6 time card
7 forklift
8 pallet

FIRST AID

9 conveyor belt
10 safety goggles
11 first-aid kit
12 fire extinguisher
13 hand truck
14 warehouse
15 loading dock / bay
16 freight lift
17 foreman

What are time cards?
They're cards that show how many hours a worker works.

What's a warehouse?
It's a place where things are stored.

A What are ....? / What's a
...................?
B They're / It's a .... that / where
....

Questions for discussion
1 Which of these objects are used for carrying things?
2 Which of these things are necessary for safety?

1 crane
2 scaffolding
3 ladder
4 construction worker
5 hard hat
6 tool belt
7 girder
8 hook
9 excavation site
10 dumper truck
11 cement mixer
12 cement
13 digger / excavator
14 ear protectors / defenders
15 wheelbarrow
16 pneumatic drill
17 brick
18 trowel
19 bulldozer
20 sledgehammer
21 two-way radio
22 spirit level
23 pickaxe
24 shovel

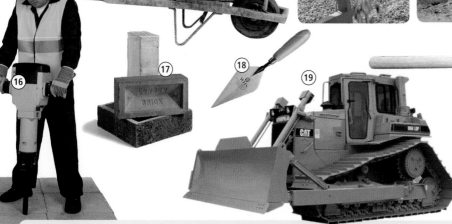

Have you ever used a shovel?
Yes, I have.

Have you ever operated a crane?
No, I haven't.

A Have you ever used / operated a ....?
B Yes, I have. No, I haven't.

Questions for discussion
1 Which of these things do people drive?
2 Which of these things make a lot of noise?
3 Which of these things could a person carry?

1 three-star hotel
2 chambermaid
3 foyer
4 checking in
5 reception
6 checking out
7 receptionist
8 guest
9 concierge
10 bar
11 restaurant

12 lift,
    elevator *AmE*
13 porter
14 suitcase
15 double room
16 bathroom
17 twin room
18 room key
19 trouser press
20 room service
21 conference
   room

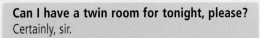

Can I have a twin room for tonight, please?
Certainly, sir.

Can I check out, please?
Certainly, madam.

A Can I ....,
  please?
B ....

Questions for discussion

1 What's the difference between checking in and checking out?

2 You are staying in a five-star hotel. What would you expect to have in the hotel and your room?

1 suspect
2 police officer
3 handcuffs
4 evidence
5 courtroom
6 witness
7 court reporter
8 judge
9 barrister
10 jury
11 defendant
12 guard

13 solicitor
14 prison
15 prison officer
16 inmate
17 verdict

The Daily Reporter
GUILTY!

Who helps a crime suspect?
A solicitor.

Who listens to the evidence in a courtroom?
The judge and jury.

A **Who gives evidence in a courtroom?**
B A ....

A Who ....?
B A / The ....

Questions for discussion

1 Is the legal system in your country the same as this?

2 What can people do to protect themselves and their property?

1 head
2 arm
3 back
4 waist
5 buttocks
6 leg
7 face
8 chest
9 stomach
10 hip
11 hand
12 foot
13 eye
14 nose
15 mouth
16 chin
17 hair
18 ear
19 lips
20 neck

21 nail
22 thumb
23 finger
24 wrist

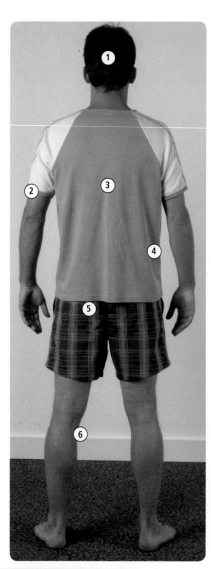

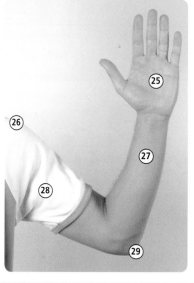

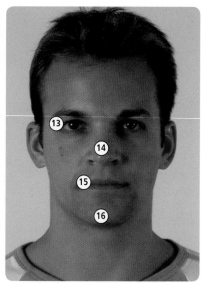

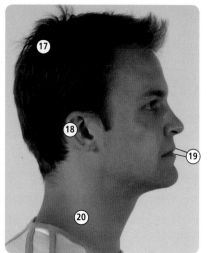

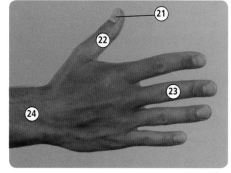

25 palm
26 shoulder
27 forearm
28 upper arm
29 elbow

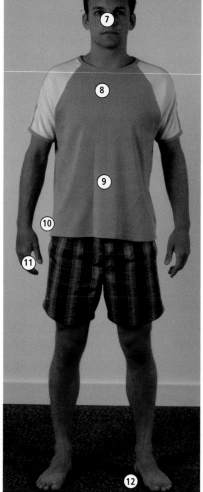

30 knee
31 thigh
32 shin
33 calf
34 ankle
35 toe
36 heel

Have you ever broken your wrist?
Yes, I broke it a few years ago.

Have you ever injured your back?
No, never.

A **Have you ever broken your ankle?**
B ....

A **Have you ever broken / injured your**........................?
B ....

Questions for discussion

1 What are the five senses and which body part is used by each?

2 Some of these words are used in different contexts, e.g., a chair has arms, legs and a back. Can you think of other examples?

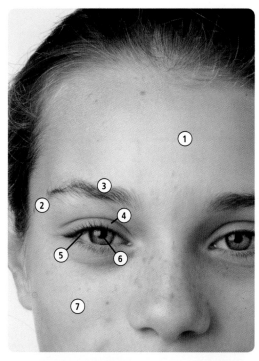

1 forehead
2 temple
3 eyebrow
4 eyelid
5 eyelash
6 pupil
7 cheek

8 tongue
9 tooth

10 brain
11 throat
12 vein
13 artery
14 lung
15 heart
16 liver
17 stomach
18 kidney
19 small intestine
20 large intestine
21 fatty tissue
22 muscles

23 skeleton
24 skull
25 breastbone
26 ribs
27 spine / backbone
28 pelvis / hip-bone
29 kneecap

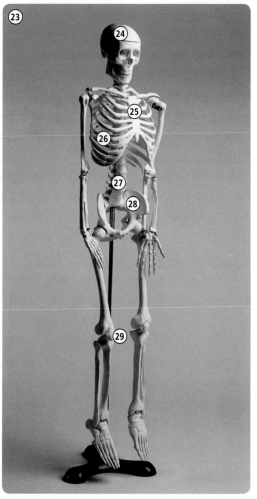

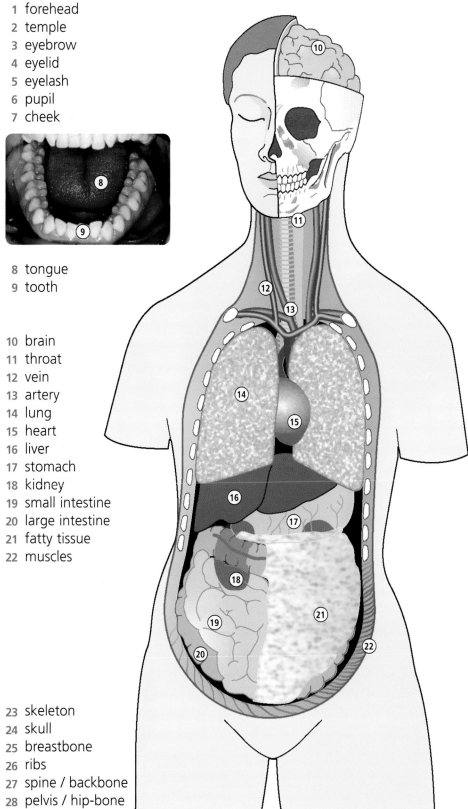

PHYSICAL DESCRIPTIONS

1 black hair
2 blond / fair hair
3 red / ginger hair
4 brown / dark hair
5 long hair
6 short hair
7 shoulder-length hair
8 shaved / cropped hair
9 straight hair
10 wavy hair
11 curly hair

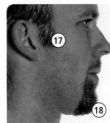

12 pony tail
13 plait
14 braids
15 parting
16 fringe
17 sideburns
18 goatee
19 stubble

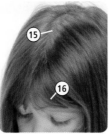

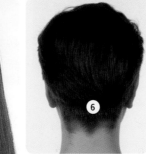
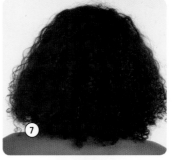

20 moustache
21 beard
22 bald
23 short
24 tall
25 slim
26 overweight

What does she look like? (11)
She's got curly, shoulder-length hair.

What does he look like? (25)
He's slim and tall, and he's got short, blond hair.

A What does she look like? (3)
B She ....

A What does he / she look like?
B He / She ....

Questions for discussion

1 What do you look like?
2 Are you happy with the way you look?

1 fall
2 talk / speak
3 touch
4 stand
5 lie down
6 hug
7 wave
8 cry
9 sit
10 smile
11 laugh

12 carry
13 frown
14 dance
15 sing
16 point
17 shake hands
18 kiss
19 push
20 pull
21 clap

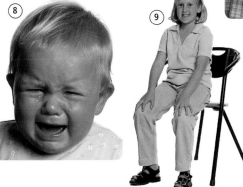

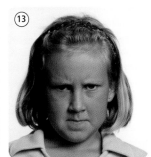

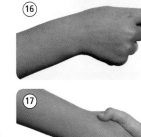

What's he doing? (8)
He's crying.

What are they doing? (17)
They're shaking hands.

A **What's he / she doing? / What are they doing?**

B He / She's .... / They're ....

Questions for discussion

1 What do you do when you're excited?

2 What do you do when you're unhappy?

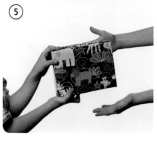

1 read
2 pick up
3 put down
4 write
5 give
6 take

7 draw
8 cut
9 glue
10 press
11 tear
12 fold
13 paint
14 open

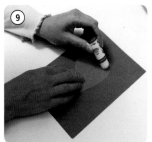

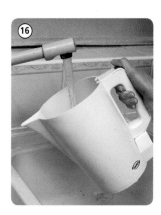

15 hold
16 fill
17 pour
18 stir
19 break

Give me that bag.

Don't open your book.

Fold the paper, but don't cut it.

A Take a piece of paper. Pick up your pen. Draw a tree. Don't write your name.

Questions for discussion

1 Do you know how to make simple origami? Try to give some instructions.

2 How do you make tea or coffee? Take turns to give and follow instructions.

1 assistant
2 wash / shampoo
3 rinse
4 washbasin
5 hairdresser
6 towel dry
7 gown
8 cut
9 blow-dry
10 mirror
11 highlights
12 style
13 hair colour
14 perm
15 braiding

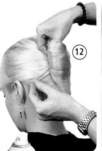

16 beading
17 styling mousse
18 hairspray
19 hair wax
20 roller

21 comb
22 hairbrush
23 styling brush
24 hairdryer
25 hand mirror
26 scissors

27 height-adjustable chair
28 footrest
29 couch
30 beautician
31 hot wax
32 (neck and shoulder) massage
33 facial
34 towel

What's hairspray used for?
It's used for fixing hairstyles.

What are scissors used for?
They're used for cutting hair.

A What are rollers used for?
B They're used for ....

A What's (a) / What are .... used for?
B It's / They're used for ....

Questions for discussion
1 What does the hairdresser usually do to your hair?
2 Which of these things do you have at home?

HAIRSTYLING, MAKE-UP AND MANICURE

A COSMETICS / MAKE-UP

1 eyeliner
2 eyebrow pencil
3 eye shadow
4 base / foundation
5 blusher / rouge
6 brush
7 lipstick
8 mascara
9 moisturiser

B MANICURE ITEMS

10 nail clippers
11 nail scissors
12 emery board
13 nail file
14 nail polish / varnish

C TOILETRIES

15 electric shaver
16 shaving gel
17 aftershave
18 razor
19 razor blade
20 shampoo
21 conditioner
22 perfume
23 cologne
24 tweezers
25 comb
26 hairbrush
27 hairdryer

How often do you use eye shadow?
I never use eye shadow.
I often use eye shadow.

A How often do you use (a) ....?
B I never / rarely / sometimes / often / always use (a) ....

Questions for discussion

1 Which of these things are commonly used by both men and women?

2 Which of these things usually smell nice?

1 she's got toothache
2 she's got stomachache
3 he's got a headache
4 he's got flu / a cold
5 he's got a sore throat
6 he's got a cough
7 he's hurt his hand
8 he's got backache
9 she's got a temperature
10 he's broken his leg
11 she's got a nose bleed
12 she's fallen over
13 he's sprained his ankle

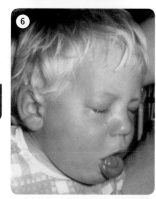

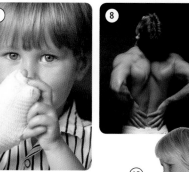
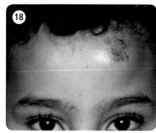
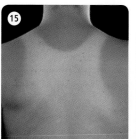
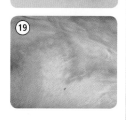
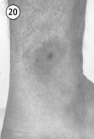

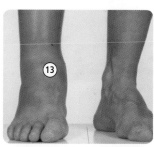
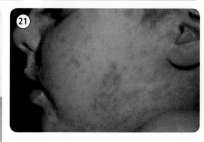

14 bruise
15 sunburn
16 scratch
17 cut
18 graze
19 scar
20 insect bite
21 rash
22 black eye
23 blood

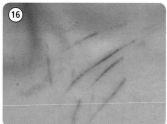
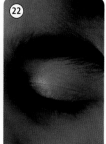

What's the matter with her? (2)
She's got stomachache.

What's wrong with him? (10)
He's broken his leg.

A What's the matter /
    What's wrong with him / her?
B He / She's ....

Questions for discussion
1 When was the last time you were ill? What was the matter?
2 What's the best way to stay healthy?

MEDICINE: AT THE CHEMIST'S

For irritated eyes
1 eye drops

For a cough
2 throat lozenges
3 cough mixture

For an insect bite
4 cream
5 spray

For hayfever / allergy
6 antihistamine tablets

For a cold
7 cold remedy
8 tissues

For cracked lips
9 lip balm

For a temperature
10 thermometer

For a headache
11 painkiller

For stomachache
12 antacid / Alka-Seltzer™

For a cut
13 (sticking) plaster

For a graze
14 gauze (pad)
15 plasters

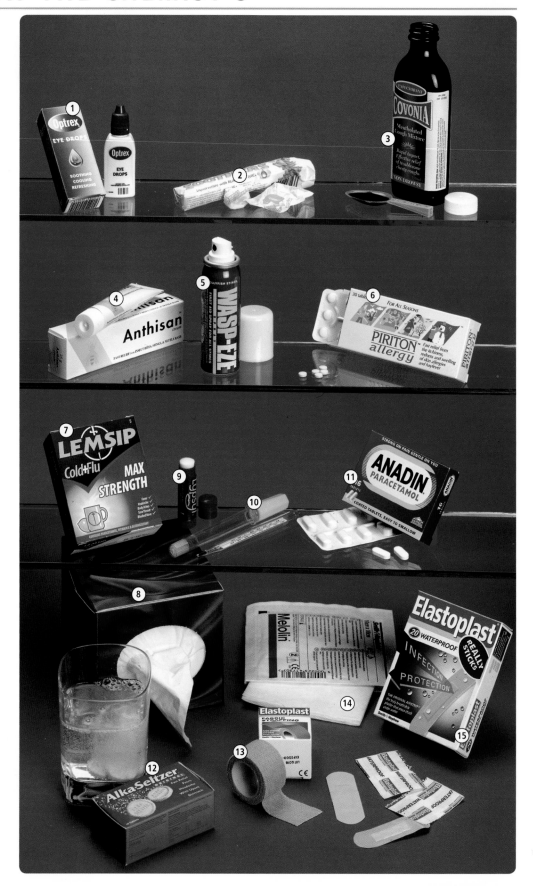

I've got a cough.
You should take some cough medicine.

I've got a cut.
You should use some plaster.

A **I've got irritated eyes.**
B You should use ....

A **I've got (a / an)** ....
B You should take / use some / a / an
....

Questions for discussion
1 Which of these things do you have at home?
2 Which of these things would you take on holiday with you?

THE DOCTOR'S SURGERY

1 doctor / general practitioner (GP)
2 X-ray
3 examination couch
4 patient
5 height chart
6 scales
7 nurse
8 medical records
9 blood pressure gauge
10 prescription
11 stethoscope

MEDICAL SPECIALISTS

12 cardiologist
13 osteopath
14 ear, nose, throat specialist
15 paediatrician
16 physiotherapist
17 obstetrician / gynaecologist
18 ophthalmologist
19 chiropodist
20 counsellor / therapist
21 dietician
22 dermatologist

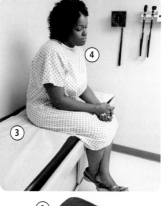

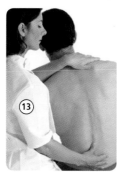

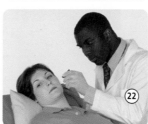

Metres
3
2.5
2
1.5

What's a cardiologist?
A cardiologist is a doctor who treats problems of the heart.

A What's a / an ....?
B A .... is a .... who / that ....

Questions for discussion
1 When do you go to your doctor's surgery?
2 Have you ever visited any of these specialists?

A HOSPITAL WARD

1 nurse
2 consultant
3 patient
4 waiting room
5 (hospital) trolley
6 (hospital) porter
7 X-rays
8 injection
9 needle
10 syringe
11 scanner
12 stitches
13 crutch
14 plaster cast
15 sling
16 surgical collar
17 wheelchair
18 medical chart

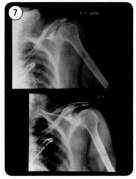

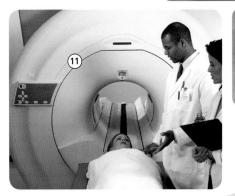
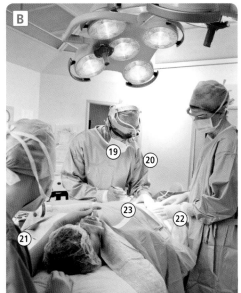

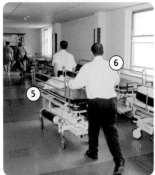
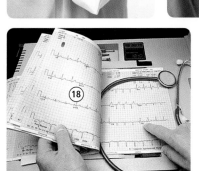

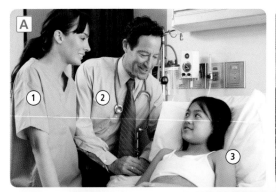

B OPERATING THEATRE

19 mask
20 surgeon
21 anaesthetist
22 surgical glove
23 operation
24 scalpel

Why are you wearing a plaster cast?
Because I broke my arm.

Why did they give you a surgical collar?
Because I hurt my neck.

A Why are you wearing / using
..............................? / **Why did
they give you** ....?
B Because ....

Questions for discussion
What happens if you go to hospital with:
1 a broken leg?
2 a bad cut on your arm?

1 dentist
2 dental nurse
3 patient
4 lamp
5 (oral) hygienist
6 basin
7 drill
8 dentures
9 orthodontist
10 mouthwash
11 dental floss
12 toothpaste
13 toothbrush
14 toothpick
15 mirror
16 decay
17 tooth
18 gum
19 plaque
20 back teeth
21 front teeth
22 filling
23 brace

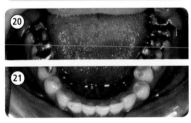
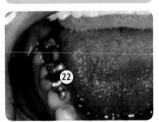

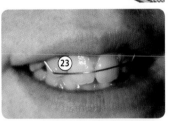
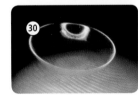

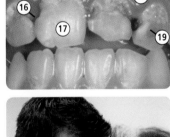
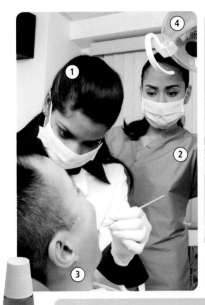
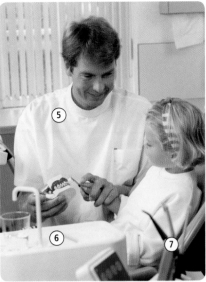

24 optician
25 alphabet board
26 glasses case
27 frame
28 lens
29 glasses
30 contact lens
31 cleaning fluid
32 eye drops

How often do you see a dentist?
Three times a year.

How often do you use mouthwash?
Once a day.

A **How often do you use eye drops?**
B Twice a year.

A **How often do you** ....?
B Once / Twice / Three times a ....
/ Never.

Questions for discussion
1 When did you last visit a dentist?
2 What did he / she do?
3 Do you regularly visit an optician?

MEN'S AND WOMEN'S WEAR 1

OUTDOOR CLOTHING
1 anorak
2 coat
3 umbrella
4 raincoat
5 cagoule
6 jacket
7 scarf
8 gloves
9 fleece

HATS
10 hat
11 baseball cap
12 sunhat
13 rainhat
14 beret

SWEATERS
15 crewneck jumper / sweater
16 poloneck jumper / sweater
17 V-neck jumper / sweater
18 cardigan
19 hooded top / hoodie

Do you prefer coats or jackets?
I prefer jackets.

Do you prefer sweaters or cardigans?
I prefer sweaters.

A Do you prefer .... or ....?
B I prefer ....

Questions for discussion
1 Which of these things do you need in wet or cold weather?
2 Which of these things do you have at home?

FOOTWEAR

1 walking boots
2 boots
3 wellingtons, wellies
4 shoes
5 trainers, sneakers *AmE*
6 court shoes, pumps *AmE*
7 sandals
8 slippers
9 flip-flops, thongs *AmE*

FORMAL WEAR

10 suit
11 jacket
12 blouse
13 skirt
14 dress
15 cocktail dress
16 evening gown / ball gown

NIGHTCLOTHES

17 nightdress / nightie
18 dressing gown
19 pyjamas
20 bathrobe

UNDERWEAR

21 ankle socks
22 slip
23 bra
24 knickers, panties *AmE*
25 camisole
26 tights
27 stockings

What colour is the evening gown?
It's blue.

What colour are the ankle socks?
They're blue and black.

A What colour is / are the
.............................?
B It's / They're (light / dark)
....

Questions for discussion

1 Which of these things are only worn at home?
2 In your opinion, which type of clothes look best on a woman?

MEN'S AND WOMEN'S WEAR 3

CASUAL WEAR

1 sweatshirt
2 jeans
3 top
4 leggings
5 T-shirt
6 shorts
7 jacket
8 skirt
9 vest

UNDERWEAR

10 socks
11 vest / undershirt
12 (boxer) shorts
13 underpants

FORMAL WEAR

14 suit
15 jacket
16 shirt
17 tie

18 trousers, pants *AmE*
19 tuxedo / dinner jacket
20 bow tie
21 waistcoat

CASUAL WEAR

22 sweatshirt
23 jeans
24 T-shirt
25 shorts
26 dungarees
27 polo shirt
28 trousers, pants *AmE*
29 jacket

What's she wearing? (1) (2)
She's wearing a purple sweatshirt and jeans.

What's he wearing? (27) (28)
He's wearing a red polo shirt and light-coloured trousers.

A What's he wearing? (24) (25)
B He's wearing a .... and ....

A What's he / she wearing?
B He's / She's wearing .... and
....

Questions for discussion

1 Describe the clothes that you usually wear.

2 Which type of clothes look best on a man?

SPORTSWEAR

1 tracksuit
2 cycling shorts
3 bikini
4 singlet / running vest
5 running shorts
6 swimming trunks
7 swimming costume / swimsuit

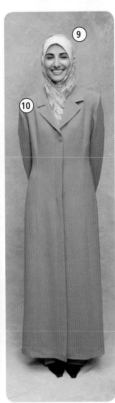

OTHER TYPES OF CLOTHING

8 kaftan
9 hijab / headscarf
10 jilbab
11 sari
12 African dress
13 shalwar kameez
14 kurta
15 kilt
16 turban

DESCRIBING CLOTHES

PARTS OF CLOTHES AND SHOES

1 lapel
2 collar
3 sleeve
4 hood
5 shoelace
6 buckle
7 heel
8 sole
9 hemline
10 button
11 buttonhole
12 pocket

13 seam
14 zip
15 cuff
16 waistband

SHAPES

17 short-sleeved
18 long-sleeved
19 wide
20 narrow
21 loose
22 tight
23 baggy

Can a dress have pockets?
Yes, it can.

Can shorts have a hood?
No, they can't.

A Can (a) .... have
.............................?
B Yes, it / they can. / No, it / they can't.

Questions for discussion

1 Do you prefer shoes with high heels or low heels?
2 Do you prefer jackets with wide or narrow lapels?
3 Do you prefer long-sleeved or short-sleeved shirts?

COLOURS

1 white
2 light blue
3 yellow
4 navy blue
5 camel
6 pink
7 brown
8 green
9 purple
10 beige
11 cream
12 blue
13 red
14 grey
15 orange
16 black
17 turquoise

PATTERNS

18 striped
19 spotted
20 patterned
21 plain
22 tartan
23 checked

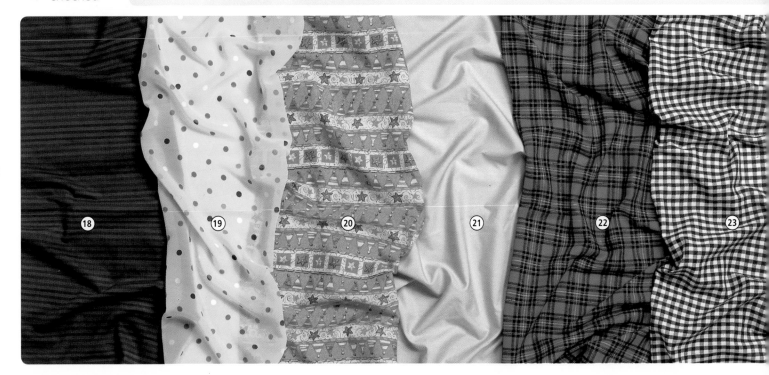

Which colours do you like?
Yellow and red.

Which fabric do you like?
The tartan one.

A Which .... do you like?
B The .... one (and the
.... one).

Questions for discussion

1 Which of these colours and patterns do you often wear?

2 Describe what the person next to you is wearing.

1 pattern
2 iron-on tape
3 Velcro™
4 scissors
5 needle
6 thread
7 sewing basket
8 tape measure
9 pin cushion
10 wool
11 knitting needle
12 thimble
13 hook and eye
14 press stud (popper)
15 polyester
16 denim
17 cotton
18 leather
19 wool
20 linen
21 silk

22 sewing machine
23 safety pin
24 sequins
25 pin
26 rip / tear
27 stain
28 dressmaker
29 tailor
30 broken zip
31 missing button

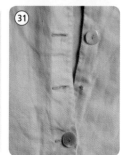

What is Velcro™ used for?
It's used to join two pieces of fabric together.

What are sequins used for?
They're used to decorate fabrics.

A What is / are (a)
.... used for?
B It's / They're used to
....

Questions for discussion
1 Which of the things do you have at home?
2 What should you do for each of the problems (26, 27, 30, 31)?

A JEWELLERY

1 money clip
2 cuff link
3 tie clip
4 watch
5 handkerchief
6 chain
7 brooch
8 necklace
9 earring
10 ring
11 pearls
12 hair slide
13 bracelet

B METALS

14 gold
15 silver

C GEMS

16 diamond
17 emerald
18 ruby
19 amethyst
20 sapphire
21 topaz

D ACCESSORIES

22 braces, suspenders *AmE*
23 shoulder bag
24 document case
25 Filofax™ / personal organiser
26 make-up bag
27 shopping bag
28 handbag
29 clutch bag
30 key ring
31 scarf
32 briefcase
33 wallet
34 purse
35 belt
36 buckle

That's a nice tie.
I agree. / I disagree. I don't like it.

Those are nice earrings.
I agree. / I disagree. I don't like them.

A That's a nice / Those are nice
....
B I agree / disagree. I don't like it / them.

Questions for discussion
In your opinion, which of these things:
1 are expensive?
2 are useful?

EDUCATION IN GREAT BRITAIN

Stages in Education

Foundation:	ages 3 to end of reception nursery or pre-school	
Primary (children aged 5 to 11)		
Key Stage 1	Year 1	5–6 years old
	Year 2	6–7 years old
Key Stage 2	Year 3	7–8 years old
	Year 4	8–9 years old
	Year 5	9–10 years old
	Year 6	10–11 years old

Secondary (students aged 11 to 18)		**Qualifications**
Key Stage 3	Year 7 11–12 years old	
	Year 8 12–13 years old	
	Year 9 13–14 years old	
Key Stage 4	Year 10 14–15 years old	GCSE (General Certificate of Secondary Education)
	Year 11 15–16 years old	GNVQ (General National Vocational Qualification)
Key Stage 5	(non compulsory)	
	Year 12 16–17 years old	AS-level (Advanced Subsidary), A-level (Advanced
	Year 13 17–18 years old	Level)

1 nursery school / pre-school
2 primary school

3 secondary school
4 boarding school
5 dormitory
6 A-level student

7 university
8 university graduates

University Qualifications

Undergraduate qualifications (after 2–4 years)	HND	Higher National Diploma
	Dip HE	Diploma of Higher Education
	BA	Bachelor of Arts
	BSc	Bachelor of Science
	BEd	Bachelor of Education
Postgraduate qualifications (2 years + after the first degree)	PGCE	Postgraduate Certificate of Education
	MA	Master of Arts
	MSc	Master of Science
	MEd	Master of Education
	MBA	Master of Business Administration
	MPhil	Master of Philosophy
	PhD	Doctor of Philosophy

The tables show a simplified structure and only the main qualifications.

1 kite
2 swings
3 roundabout
4 scooter
5 slide
6 tricycle
7 bench
8 doll's pram
9 sandpit
10 sand
11 climbing frame
12 seesaw
13 skateboard
14 roller skates
15 doll

16 pre-school
17 toy
18 colouring book
19 book
20 crayons
21 paintbrush
22 paintbox
23 rounded scissors
24 glue
25 building blocks / bricks
26 jigsaw puzzle
27 easel

What colour is the scooter?
It's blue and yellow.

What colour are the building blocks?
They're yellow, red, green and blue.

A **What colour is/are the
........................?**
B It's/They're ....

Questions for discussion

1 Which of these games are usually played indoors?

2 Which of these things did you like playing with / on when you were little?

THE SCHOOL

THE CLASSROOM
1 compass
2 exercise book
3 ruler
4 pencil
5 pencil sharpener
6 rubber
7 protractor
8 set-square
9 (ballpoint) pen / biro™
10 calculator

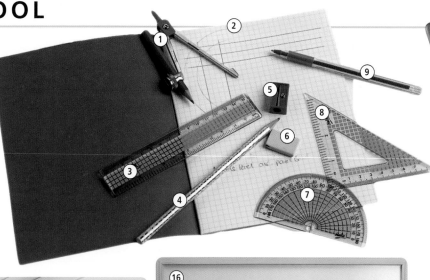

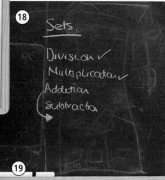

11 teacher
12 desk
13 textbook
14 pupil
15 wall chart
16 whiteboard
17 whiteboard marker
18 blackboard
19 chalk

Read chapter one pages 8-13

Write your comments on these pages.

Discussion:

Groups - 2 or 3 people.

Role play.

Sets.

Division ✓
Multiplication ✓
Addition
Subtraction

TECHNOLOGY IN THE CLASSROOM
30 CD player
31 DVD player
32 computer
33 language lab booth
34 overhead projector

THE SCIENCE LAB
20 measuring cylinder
21 test tubes
22 safety glasses
23 pipette
24 measuring beaker
25 bunsen burner
26 tongs

THE GYM
27 wall bars
28 mat
29 (pommel) horse

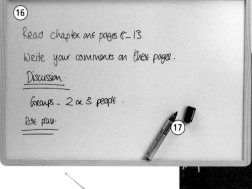

PRIMARY SCHOOL AND SECONDARY SCHOOL

1 maths
2 science
3 music
4 PE (physical education)
5 history
6 English
7 RE (religious education)
8 art
9 geography
10 IT (information technology)
11 PCSE / citizenship

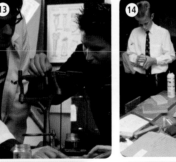

SECONDARY SCHOOL ONLY

12 chemistry
13 physics
14 design and technology
15 biology
16 performing arts (drama)
17 sociology
18 business studies
19 Latin
20 Spanish
21 French
22 German

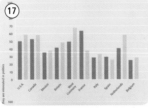

Do you like science at school?
No, I don't.

Did you like music at school?
Yes, I did.

A Do / Did you like .... at school?

B Yes, I do. / No, I don't. / Yes, I did. / No, I didn't.

Questions for discussion

1 What subjects do schoolchildren study in your country?

2 What exams do they take in your country?

COLLEGE, ADULT EDUCATION, LIBRARY

A TUTORIAL

1 lecturer's / tutor's office
2 tutor

B CAMPUS

3 student welfare office
4 cafeteria

C LECTURE

5 lecture hall
6 lecturer

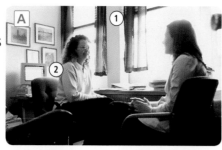

D LIBRARY

7 reference section	10 lending desk	13 librarian	17 library card	21 microfiche reader
8 information section	11 shelves	14 encyclopedia	18 periodical section	22 library assistant
9 information desk	12 public Internet computer	15 dictionary	19 journal	23 photocopier
		16 atlas	20 microfiche	

What's a microfiche?
It's a sheet of microfilm that can contain many pages of printed materials.

What's an information desk?
It's a place where students can ask the librarian for help.

A What's a cafeteria?
B ....

A What's a / an ....?
B It's a / an .... that / where / who ....

Questions for discussion
What must you do in a library if you want to:
1 take out a book?
2 look for some information?

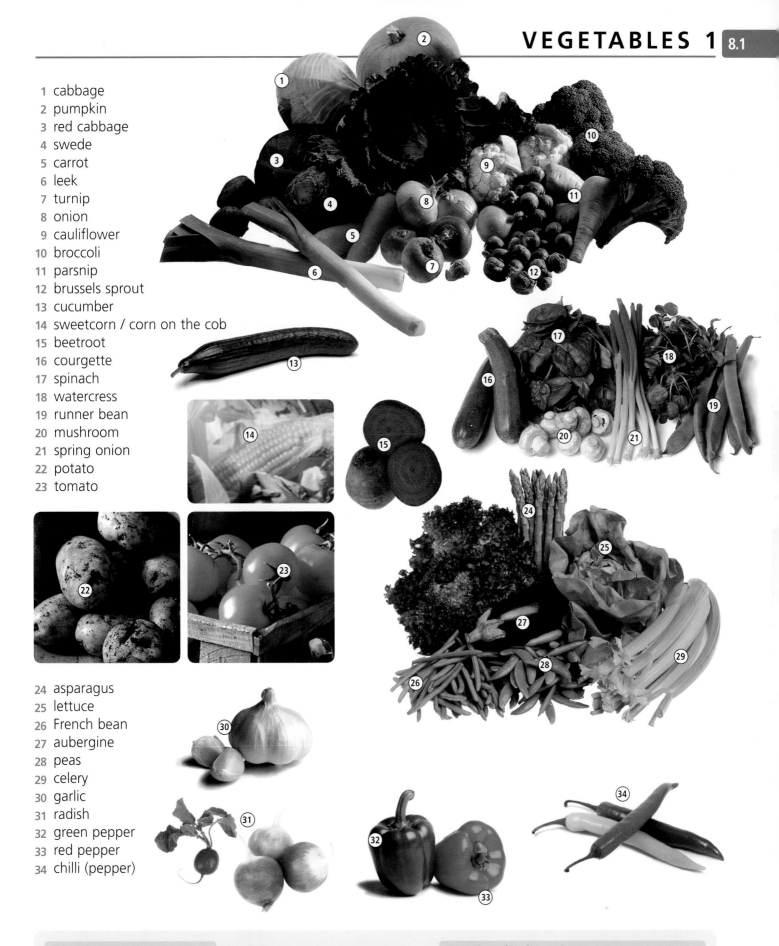

1 cabbage
2 pumpkin
3 red cabbage
4 swede
5 carrot
6 leek
7 turnip
8 onion
9 cauliflower
10 broccoli
11 parsnip
12 brussels sprout
13 cucumber
14 sweetcorn / corn on the cob
15 beetroot
16 courgette
17 spinach
18 watercress
19 runner bean
20 mushroom
21 spring onion
22 potato
23 tomato

24 asparagus
25 lettuce
26 French bean
27 aubergine
28 peas
29 celery
30 garlic
31 radish
32 green pepper
33 red pepper
34 chilli (pepper)

Do you ever buy watercress?
Yes, I do.

Do you ever grow tomatoes?
No, I don't.

A **Do you ever buy / grow / eat**
.........................?
B Yes, I do. / No, I don't.

Questions for discussion
1 Which of these vegetables grow in your country or region?
2 Which can you eat without cooking?

1 broad bean
2 butternut squash
3 celeriac
4 fennel
5 sweet potato
6 yam
7 okra
8 pak choi
9 artichoke
10 jerusalem artichoke

FRESH HERBS

11 basil
12 chives
13 coriander
14 dill
15 parsley
16 rosemary
17 mint
18 oregano
19 sage
20 tarragon

1 grapefruit
2 satsuma
3 clementine
4 lemon
5 lime
6 orange
7 tangerine

8 blackcurrant
9 redcurrant
10 cherry
11 starfruit
12 papaya
13 pineapple
14 mango
15 melon
16 gooseberry
17 blueberry

18 lychee
19 grape
20 avocado
21 kiwi fruit
22 banana

23 pear
24 apple
25 plum
26 strawberry

27 peach
28 raspberry
29 rhubarb
30 nectarine
31 watermelon
32 apricot
33 pomegranate
34 guava
35 passion fruit
36 cranberries

37 hazelnut
38 walnut
39 Brazil nut
40 coconut
41 cashew nut
42 peanut

43 raisin
44 fig
45 prune
46 date

Do you prefer apples or pears?
I prefer pears.

What's your favourite fruit?
I love blueberries.

A **Do you prefer** .... **or**
.... **?**
B I prefer .... / I don't like either.

A **What's your favourite fruit?**
B I love ....

Questions for discussion

1 Which of these fruits grow in your country or region?

2 Which of these fruits are available in your country throughout the year?

CHECKOUT AREA

1 cashier
2 customer / shopper
3 conveyor belt
4 trolley
5 aisle
6 self-checkout area
7 carrier bag / shopping bag
8 shopping
9 checkout desk

FROZEN FOODS

10 pizza
11 chips
12 ice cream
13 fish fingers
14 peas
15 burgers

DAIRY PRODUCTS

16 milk
17 cream
18 cheese
19 butter
20 eggs
21 yoghurt / yogurt
22 margarine

TINNED / BOTTLED FOOD

23 sweetcorn
24 baked beans
25 corned beef
26 soup
27 tuna
28 honey
29 chopped tomatoes
30 jam

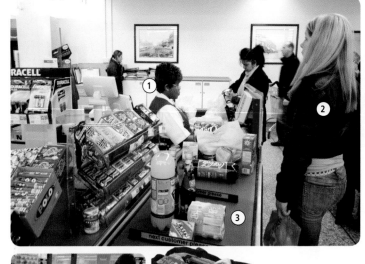

DRY GOODS

1 pasta
2 couscous
3 rice
4 coffee
5 cocoa
6 herbal tea
7 tea
8 biscuits
9 oats
10 flour
11 cereal

CONDIMENTS

12 mayonnaise
13 sugar
14 ketchup
15 vinegar
16 mustard
17 salad dressing
18 herbs and spices
19 oil
20 salt
21 pepper

HOUSEHOLD PRODUCTS

29 bin bags
30 dog food
31 cat food
32 washing powder
33 washing capsules
34 washing liquid
35 washing-up liquid

DRINKS

22 white wine
23 beer
24 red wine
25 lemonade
26 orange juice
27 cola
28 mineral water

What do we need today?
We need some biscuits and some washing powder, but we don't need any bin bags.

A What do we need today?

B We need ...., but we don't need ....

B We need some ...., but we don't need any ....

Questions for discussion

What would you buy to:

1 make breakfast?
2 do some washing?

SUPERMARKET COUNTERS

MEAT

1 sausage
2 minced beef
3 chicken leg
4 bacon
5 turkey
6 leg of lamb
7 beef joint
8 pork chops
9 lamb chops
10 steak
11 liver
12 stewing beef

DELICATESSEN

13 blue cheese
14 Swiss cheese
15 brie
16 coleslaw
17 hummous
18 taramasalata
19 smoked ham
20 ham
21 pie
22 kabanos
23 salami
24 chorizo

FISH AND SEAFOOD

25 whole trout
26 salmon steaks
27 cod fillet
28 prawns
29 lobster
30 crab
31 mussels

BAKERY

32 wholemeal bread
33 bagel
34 cake
35 white bread
36 pitta bread
37 baguette
38 naan bread

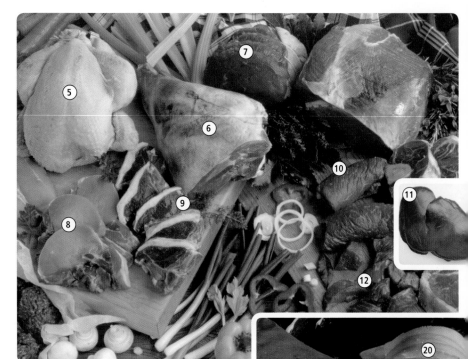
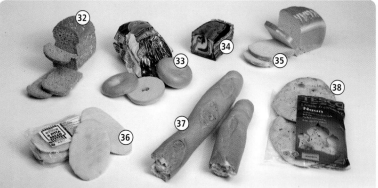

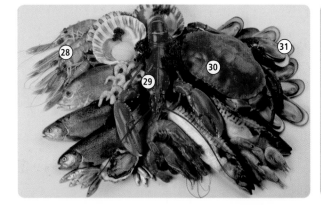

1 waiter 3 wine list
2 menu 4 dessert trolley

STARTERS / HORS D'ŒUVRES

5 tomato soup
6 melon and parma ham
7 chicken liver pâté
8 prawn cocktail
9 smoked salmon
10 blini
11 borscht
12 dim sum
13 hot and sour soup

WINE LIST

	Per bottle
White	
Australian Chardonnay	£15.99
New Zealand Sauvignon Blanc	£13.99
House White	£11.99
Red	£15.99
Australian Shiraz	£13.99
Cotes Du Rhone	£11.99
House Red	
House Champagne	£27.99

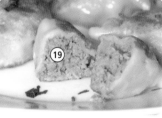

MAIN COURSES

14 stuffed peppers
15 roast beef with Yorkshire pudding
16 lasagne
17 fillet of sole
18 chicken tikka masala
19 pierogi
20 shashlik
21 stuffed vine leaves
22 pad thai
23 sweet and sour chicken with rice
24 moussaka
25 fajitas
26 tortilla
27 nacho chips
28 bigos
29 koftas

AT THE RESTAURANT 2

SIDE VEGETABLES

1 roast potatoes
2 mixed vegetables
3 carrots
4 sweetcorn
5 peas
6 side salad

DESSERTS

7 cream
8 ice cream
9 cheesecake
10 (chocolate) gateau
11 tiramisu
12 panna cotta
13 apple pie
14 halva
15 baklava
16 turkish delight

DRINKS

17 coffee
18 tea
19 milk
20 fizzy mineral water
21 still mineral water
22 white wine
23 champagne
24 red wine

Are you ready to order?
Yes, I'd like tomato soup and moussaka, please.

What would you like to drink?
Some red wine, please.

Are you ready to order?
Yes, I'd like .... and ...., please.

What would you like to drink?
Some ...., please.

Questions for discussion

1 When you eat out, do you normally eat a starter, a main course and dessert?

2 Which of the foods on the last two pages would you eat?

1 mustard
2 tomato ketchup
3 sachet of pepper
4 sachet of salt
5 (paper) napkin
6 cola
7 cheeseburger
8 beefburger / hamburger
9 straw
10 milk shake
11 fizzy drink
12 orange juice
13 smoothie
14 hot dog
15 chips / French fries
16 cone
17 ice cream

18 gherkins
19 olives
20 peanuts
21 crisps, chips *AmE*
22 nuts and raisins

23 doughnut
24 muffin
25 fish and chips
26 vinegar
27 fried chicken
28 ploughman's lunch
29 sweets, candy *AmE*

30 chicken wrap
31 sausage roll
32 baked potato
33 sushi
34 falafel
35 shish kebab
36 doner kebab
37 samosa

Would you like a hot dog?
Yes, please.

Would you like some sushi?
No, thanks.

A Would you like some ketchup?
B Yes, please. / No, thanks.

A Would you like a / some
...........................?
B ....

Questions for discussion
1 Which of these things are sweet?
2 Do you dislike any of these things?
3 How often do you buy fast food?

CONTAINERS AND QUANTITIES

1 bottle
2 tin
3 packet
4 jar
5 tub / container
6 box
7 carton
8 bag
9 can
10 six-pack
11 roll
12 loaf

13 tube
14 a cupful
15 a teaspoonful
16 a tablespoonful

17 1 metre
18 1 centimetre
19 1 millimetre

20 empty
21 one quarter / a quarter
22 one third / a third
23 one half / a half
24 three quarters
25 full

26 100 grams
27 1 kilogram
28 1,000 millilitres
29 1 litre

How much milk do we want?
Four litres. / Two cartons.

How many bottles of cola do we want?
Two.

A **How much .... do we want? / How many .... of .... do we want?**

B **..................... .**

Questions for discussion

Which of these containers can be made of:

1 paper?   2 plastic?

3 glass?   4 metal?

1 cook
2 wash (salad)
3 peel (potatoes)
4 grate (cheese)
5 chop
6 crush (garlic)
7 beat (eggs)
8 cut up
9 rub in (flour and butter)
10 slice
11 grease (a tin)
12 break (an egg)
13 stir
14 mix (ingredients)
15 knead (dough)
16 steam
17 sauté
18 boil (eggs)
19 add (liquid)
20 bake
21 pour (water)
22 weigh (beans)
23 stir fry
24 grill
25 roast
26 barbecue
27 measure ingredients
28 fry (an egg)

What's he doing? (3)
He's peeling potatoes.

What's he doing? (15)
He's kneading dough.

A **What's she doing? (7)**
B She's ....

A **What's he / she doing?**
B He's / She's ....

Questions for discussion

1 In what different ways can you cook meat?

2 Explain how you make one of your favourite dishes.

BREAKFAST, LUNCH, DINNER

BREAKFAST

1 porridge
2 cereal
3 bread
4 full cream milk
5 semi-skimmed milk
6 muesli
7 grapefruit
8 tea
9 coffee
10 boiled egg
11 butter
12 toast
13 croissant
14 jam
15 marmalade
16 English breakfast

LUNCH

17 soup and bread roll
18 cheese on toast
19 ham salad
20 sandwiches

DINNER

21 spaghetti bolognese
22 shepherd's pie
23 sausage, mash and peas
24 fish fingers, chips and baked beans
25 omelette
26 pizza
27 mushroom risotto
28 tacos
29 paella
30 couscous

What would you like for breakfast?
I'd like some muesli with semi-skimmed milk, and tea, please.

What would you like for dinner?
I'd like sausage and mash, please.

A Would you like for ....?
B I'd like ....

Questions for discussion

1 What's a typical breakfast in your country?

2 What things do you usually eat for dinner?

1 railway station
2 clock
3 arrivals and departures board
4 platform entrance
5 passenger
6 train
7 engine
8 carriage
9 track
10 the Underground
11 platform
12 (return) ticket
13 second class
14 first class
15 rush hour

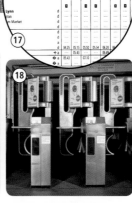

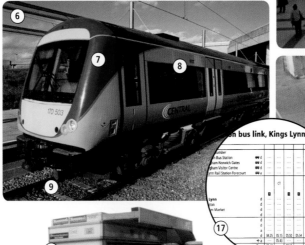

16 kiosk
17 timetable
18 barrier
19 tunnel

20 minicab
21 taxi
22 (taxi) driver
23 black cab

24 luggage compartment
25 coach
26 (bus) driver
27 bus
28 bus stop

Shall we go by train?
No, let's go by minicab.

How did you get here?
I missed the bus, so I came by taxi.

A Shall we go by ....?
B No. Let's go by ....

A How did you get here?
B I missed the ...., so I came by ....

Questions for discussion
1 Which forms of public transport do you use?
2 Are taxis quicker than going in your own car?

A CARS

1 hatchback
2 saloon car
3 estate car
4 people carrier
5 four-wheel drive
6 convertible
7 sports car

B TWO-WHEELED VEHICLES

8 motor scooter
9 bicycle
10 motorbike

C OTHER VEHICLES

11 van
12 caravan
13 minibus
14 lorry, truck *AmE*
15 tractor
16 articulated lorry
17 rickshaw

D PETROL STATION / GARAGE

18 nozzle
19 petrol pump
20 hose

E ENGINE

21 distributor
22 cylinder block
23 air filter
24 battery

1 rear windscreen
2 rearview mirror
3 brake light
4 boot
5 numberplate
6 bumper
7 exhaust pipe
8 headrest
9 seat belt
10 roof-rack
11 door
12 windscreen wiper
13 wing mirror
14 bonnet
15 headlight
16 indicator
17 sidelight
18 soft top
19 petrol cap
20 wing
21 wheel
22 tyre

23 ignition
24 dashboard
25 clutch
26 brake
27 accelerator
28 steering wheel
29 temperature gauge
30 rev counter
31 speedometer
32 fuel gauge
33 radio / cassette / CD player
34 gear lever / stick, gear shift *AmE*
35 electric window button

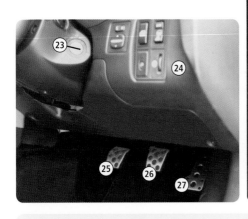

What's the matter with the car?
The exhaust pipe is broken.

What's wrong with the car?
The windscreen wipers don't work.

A **What's the matter / What's wrong with the car?**

B The .... is / are broken. /
The .... doesn't / don't work.

Questions for discussion

1 Do you have any of these vehicles?

2 What repairs has your vehicle had recently?

3 Which of these vehicles are bad for the environment?

ROAD AND ROAD SIGNS

A MOTORWAY

1 flyover
2 hard shoulder
3 inside lane
4 middle lane
5 outside lane
6 bridge

B DUAL CARRIAGEWAY

7 central reservation
8 slip road
9 cat's eyes

C JUNCTION

10 streetlight / lamp-post
11 crossroads
12 traffic lights
13 red
14 amber
15 green

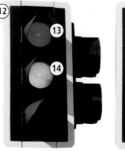

16 lorry
17 zebra crossing
18 pedestrian
19 (pedestrian) underpass

D ROUNDABOUT

20 bus
21 car

You mustn't park on the hard shoulder if you are on a motorway.

You must give way at a roundabout if a vehicle is going round it.

A You .... if the traffic lights are red.

A You must / mustn't .... if ....

Questions for discussion

1 Discuss other things you must and mustn't do if you are driving.

2 Do drivers in your country usually stop for pedestrians at zebra crossings?

E LEVEL CROSSING

22 barrier
23 railway track

F ROADWORKS

24 traffic cone

G SIGNS

25 give way sign
26 stop sign
27 road sign
28 no right turn sign
29 no U-turn sign
30 no overtaking sign
31 steep hill sign
32 no through road sign
33 cyclists only sign
34 slippery road sign
35 roadworks ahead sign
36 roundabout sign
37 level crossing sign

What does this sign mean? (30)
It means that you mustn't overtake.

What does this sign mean? (37)
It means that there's a level crossing.

A What does this sign mean?
B It means that you must /
mustn't .... /
It means that there's a /
there are ....

Questions for discussion

1 How are roads and road signs different in your country?

2 What do you think drivers and pedestrians should do to prevent road accidents?

A THE TERMINAL

1 check-in desk
2 ticket
3 departure gates
4 metal detector
5 luggage / baggage
6 porter
7 luggage trolley
8 suitcase
9 flight information screens
10 security
11 X-ray scanner
12 hand luggage
13 duty-free shop
14 passport control
15 passport
16 immigration officer

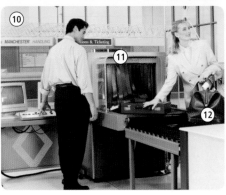

17 baggage reclaim area
18 baggage carousel
19 boarding pass
20 customs
21 customs officer

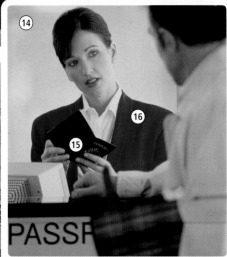

A ON BOARD

1 window
2 window seat
3 aisle seat
4 flight attendant
5 tray
6 armrest
7 cockpit
8 pilot / captain
9 instrument panel
10 co-pilot
11 oxygen mask
12 cabin
13 overhead (luggage) compartment
14 jet engine
15 life jacket

ADULT/CHILD
RFD LIFEJACKET

B THE RUNWAY

16 take-off
17 runway
18 wing
19 trailer
20 landing
21 tail
22 jet (plane)
23 rotor
24 helicopter
25 control tower
26 air traffic controller
27 hangar

What does an immigration officer do?
He or she examines passports or ID cards.

Where are the life jackets?
They're under the seats.

A What does a / an .... do?
B He or she ....

A Where is / are ....?
B It's / He's / She's / They're in / on / under / behind ....

Questions for discussion
1 What do you think is the most interesting part of the flight?
2 What are some of the reasons for flight delays?

WATER TRANSPORT

1 life jacket
2 lifeboat
3 liner / cruise ship
4 (oil) tanker
5 ferry

6 sailing ship
7 sail
8 mast
9 cable
10 anchor
11 lighthouse

12 marina
13 motor boat
14 yacht, sailboat *AmE*
15 cabin cruiser
16 cabin

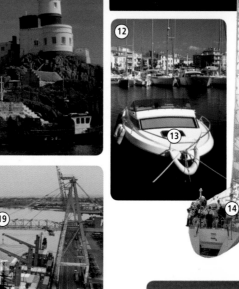

23 bow
24 stern
25 deck

17 rowing boat
18 oar

19 crane
20 ship
21 dock
22 cargo

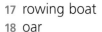

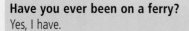

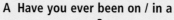

Have you ever been on a ferry?
Yes, I have.

Have you ever been in a rowing boat?
No, I haven't.

A Have you ever been on / in a
.........................?
B Yes, I have. / No, I haven't.

Questions for discussion
Which of these boats do you think is:

1 the slowest / fastest?
2 the heaviest?

1 customer
2 cashier / bank clerk
3 counter

4 cashpoint
5 cashpoint card / debit card
6 pin number
7 deposit box / slot
8 exchange rates
9 financial adviser
10 online banking

11 paying-in slip
12 credit card
13 bank statement
14 bank account number
15 bank balance
16 withdrawal slip
17 stub
18 cheque card
19 cheque
20 chequebook

21 cash
22 fifty pounds / fifty pound note
23 twenty pounds / twenty pound note
24 ten pounds / ten pound note
25 five pounds / five pound note
26 two pounds / two pound coin
27 one pound / one pound coin
28 fifty pence / fifty pence piece
29 twenty pence / twenty pence piece
30 ten pence / ten pence piece
31 five pence / five pence piece
32 two pence / two pence piece
33 one penny / one penny piece

34 traveller's cheque
35 foreign currency
36 euros
37 US dollars and cents

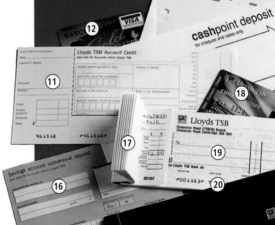

Can I have thirty pounds, please?	**A** **Can I have seventy pence, please?**
How do you want it?	**B** How do you want it?
Three ten pound notes, please.	**A** ...., please.
Here you are.	**B** ....

Questions for discussion

1 What different notes and coins are there in your country?
2 How often do you pay by credit card?

1 CCTV camera
2 road sign
3 Belisha beacon
4 zebra crossing
5 department store
6 bus
7 street
8 railings
9 offices
10 traffic
11 parking notice
12 bus shelter
13 bus stop
14 bollard
15 parking meter

16 pedestrian
17 bus lane
18 double yellow line
19 gutter
20 kerb
21 traffic lights
22 red route
23 pavement

1 skyscraper
2 tower block
3 Underground entrance
4 streetlight
5 newspaper vendor
6 newspaper stand
7 manhole cover
8 phone box
9 shop
10 flag
11 skyline
12 sky
13 river
14 bridge
15 (litter) bin
16 hoarding / billboard

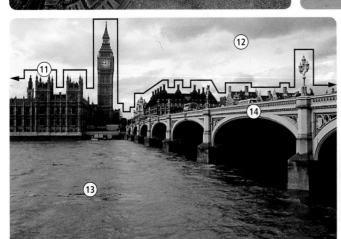
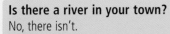

Is there a river in your town?
No, there isn't.

Are there any skyscrapers in your city?
Yes, there are.

A **Is there a / Are there any .... in your town / city?**
B Yes, there is. / No, there isn't. / Yes, there are. / No, there aren't.

Questions for discussion
1 Which of these things do you find in cities in your country?
2 What is the best thing about living in a big city?
3 What is the worst thing about living in a big city?

1 first class post
2 second class post
3 envelope
4 postmark
5 stamp
6 airmail letter
7 postcard
8 postal order
9 letter
10 (birthday) card
11 delivery
12 postman / postwoman
13 (post office) clerk
14 scales
15 counter
16 address
17 postcode
18 collection
19 pillar box
20 postbag
21 stamp machine
22 Royal Mail van
23 postbox / letterbox

24 Airsure®
25 Recorded Signed For™
26 Special Delivery™
27 scissors
28 string
29 parcel, package *AmE*
30 book of stamps

What's that? (21)
It's a stamp machine.

What are those? (7)
They're postcards.

A What's that? / What are those?
B It's a / an .... / They're
....

Questions for discussion

Imagine you are in Britain. How would you send these things:
1 a cheque to someone in your country?
2 a letter to the USA?

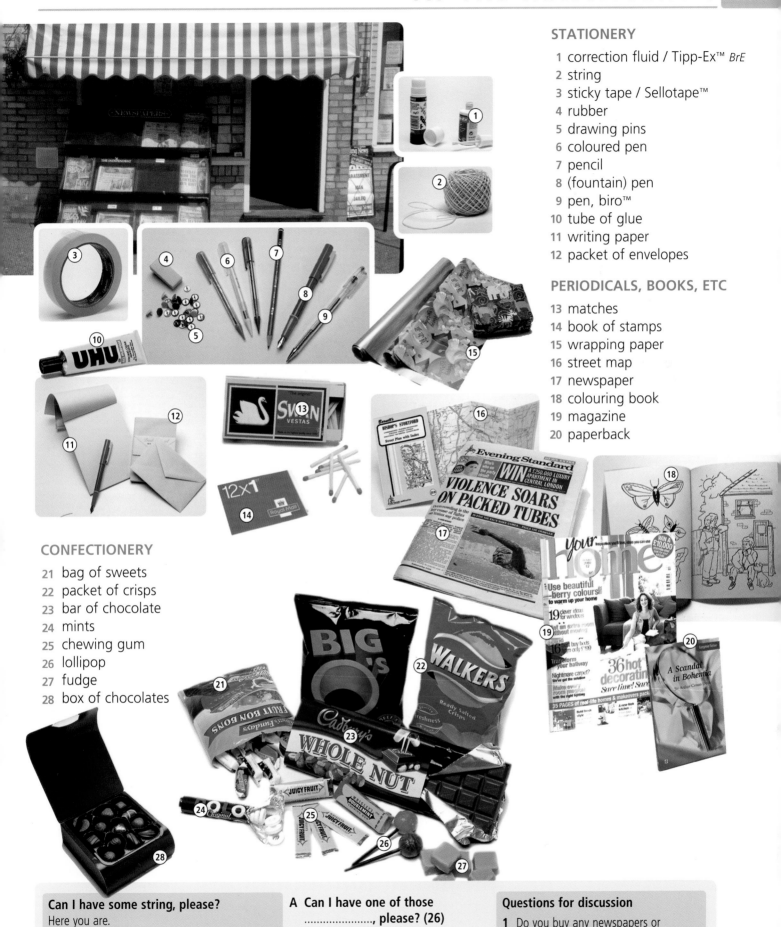

STATIONERY

1 correction fluid / Tipp-Ex™ *BrE*
2 string
3 sticky tape / Sellotape™
4 rubber
5 drawing pins
6 coloured pen
7 pencil
8 (fountain) pen
9 pen, biro™
10 tube of glue
11 writing paper
12 packet of envelopes

PERIODICALS, BOOKS, ETC

13 matches
14 book of stamps
15 wrapping paper
16 street map
17 newspaper
18 colouring book
19 magazine
20 paperback

CONFECTIONERY

21 bag of sweets
22 packet of crisps
23 bar of chocolate
24 mints
25 chewing gum
26 lollipop
27 fudge
28 box of chocolates

Can I have some string, please?
Here you are.

Can I have a packet of those crisps, please?
Here you are.

**A Can I have one of those
..................., please? (26)**
B ....

Questions for discussion

1 Do you buy any newspapers or magazines every week?

2 Do you buy any sweets every week?

1 music and entertainment shop
2 mobile phone shop
3 chemist's
4 optician's
5 sports shop
6 sweet shop
7 toy shop
8 department store

9 bookshop
10 stationer's
11 escalator
12 shoe shop
13 fabric shop
14 electronics shop
15 travel agency
16 cash machine
17 jeweller's
18 card shop
19 fashion store

Cash

I need a new laptop.
Let's go the electronics shop.

I'd like some chocolate.
Let's go to the sweet shop.

A I need some birthday cards.
B Let's go to the ....

A I need / I'd like a / an / some ....
B Let's go to the ....

Questions for discussion
1 Which of these shops do you go to every week / month?
2 Do you like or dislike shopping? Why?

POLICE

1 police station
2 police officer
3 police car

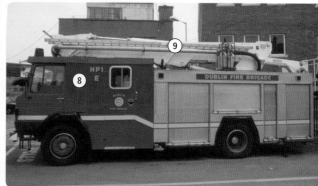

FIRE BRIGADE

4 fire
5 fire fighter
6 water
7 hose
8 fire engine
9 ladder
10 smoke
11 fire extinguisher

AMBULANCE SERVICE

12 road accident
13 injured person
14 paramedic
15 drip
16 ambulance
17 oxygen mask
18 stretcher

ROADSIDE BREAKDOWN

19 tow truck
20 roadside assistant

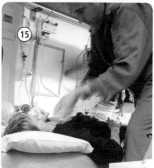

CALLING FROM A PUBLIC PHONE BOX

21 (tele)phone box
22 receiver
23 number pad
24 phonecard
25 emergency number
26 dialling code
27 international code
28 country code

In an emergency call **999**

What should you do if you see a road accident?
You should phone 999.

What should you do if you see a crime?
You should tell a police officer.

A What should you do if ....?
B You should ....

Questions for discussion

1 Have you ever been involved in an emergency situation? Describe what happened.

2 Imagine you have just seen a road accident. You phone 999 (the emergency services). Role-play the conversation with a partner.

A CRICKET

1 scoreboard
2 boundary
3 fielder
4 wicket keeper
5 cricket ball
6 wicket
7 batsman
8 (cricket) pitch
9 helmet
10 pads
11 bat
12 umpire
13 bails
14 stump
15 bowler

B FOOTBALL

16 stadium
17 crowd / fans
18 centre circle
19 halfway line
20 penalty box
21 penalty spot
22 goal
23 goal area
24 goal line
25 net
26 goalpost
27 football boots
28 yellow card
29 red card
30 referee
31 player / footballer
32 goalkeeper / goalie
33 ball

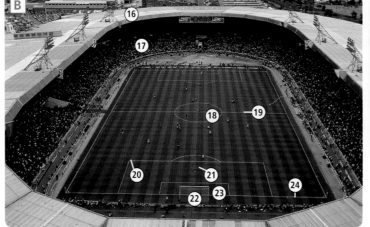

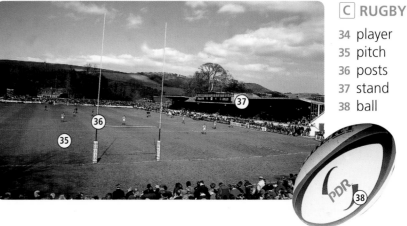

C RUGBY

34 player
35 pitch
36 posts
37 stand
38 ball

A BASKETBALL

1 backboard
2 basket
3 basketball
4 (basketball) player

B VOLLEYBALL

5 volleyball
6 net
7 (volleyball) player

C BOXING

8 glove
9 boxer
10 trunks
11 referee
12 ropes
13 ring

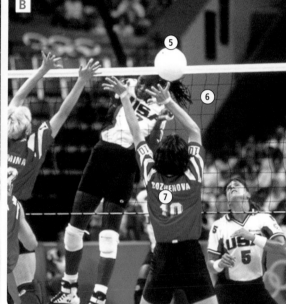

D HORSE RACING

14 gate
15 racehorse
16 jockey

Which is the best football team in Spain?
Barcelona!

A Which is the best .... team /
Who is the best .... in
.........................?
B ....

Questions for discussion
1 Do you do any of these sports?
2 Which of these sports is the most popular in your country?

INDIVIDUAL SPORTS 1

A TENNIS

1 (tennis) racket / racquet
2 (tennis) ball
3 baseline
4 (tennis) player
5 court
6 net

B SQUASH

7 (squash) player
8 (squash) racket / racquet
9 (squash) ball

C PING PONG / TABLE TENNIS

10 (ping pong) ball
11 net
12 bat
13 (ping pong) table
14 (ping pong) player

D BADMINTON

15 shuttlecock
16 (badminton) racket / racquet
17 (badminton) player

E KARATE

18 black belt

F JUDO

G WRESTLING

19 wrestler
20 mat

Would you like to try karate?
Yes, I would.

Would you like to try badminton?
I've already tried it.

A **Would you like to try** ....?
B Yes, I would. / No, I wouldn't. / I've already tried it!

Questions for discussion

1 Which of these sports do people do indoors?
2 Which of these sports are originally from Asia?

A JOGGING

1 jogger

B RUNNING

2 runner

C CYCLING

3 helmet
4 cyclist
5 wheel
6 bicycle / bike

D HORSE RIDING

7 reins
8 horse
9 rider
10 saddle
11 stirrup

E ARCHERY

12 target
13 bow
14 arrow
15 archer

F GOLF

16 golfer
17 (golf) club
18 green
19 hole
20 (golf) ball

G HANG GLIDING

21 hang glider

H ROLLERBLADING

22 helmet
23 rollerblader
24 pads
25 in-line skate / rollerblade

I PARACHUTING / SKYDIVING

26 parachutist / skydiver
27 parachute

J CLIMBING

28 climber
29 harness

K GYMNASTICS

30 gymnast
31 leotard
32 balance beam

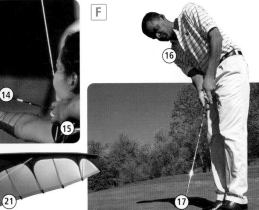

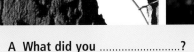

What did you do last weekend?
I did archery.
What did you do on your holiday?
I went horse riding and played golf.

A What did you ....?
B I went .... / did .... / played ....

Questions for discussion

1 Which of these sports need special clothes?
2 Choose three sports and describe what equipment you need to do them.

WATER SPORTS

A SWIMMING

1 goggles
2 swimming hat / cap
3 swimmer
4 swimming pool

B SNORKELLING

5 snorkel
6 snorkeller

C SCUBA DIVING

7 (air) tank
8 wet suit
9 mask
10 scuba diver

D DIVING

11 diver
12 diving board

E FISHING

13 (fishing) line
14 fishing rod
15 fisherman

F SURFING AND WIND-SURFING

16 sailboard
17 wind-surfer
18 surfboard
19 surfer

G ROWING

20 oar
21 rowing boat
22 oarsman / oarswoman

H CANOEING

23 paddle
24 canoeist
25 canoe

I SAILING

26 sail
27 mast
28 sailing boat / yacht, sailboat *AmE*

J WATER SKIING

29 towrope
30 motorboat
31 water skier
32 water ski

A SLEDGING

1 sledge
2 snow

B DOWNHILL SKIING

3 skier
4 pole
5 (ski) boot
6 ski
7 chairlift
8 snowboard

C SPEED SKATING

9 speed skater
10 skate
11 ice

D FIGURE SKATING

12 figure skater
13 figure skate
14 blade

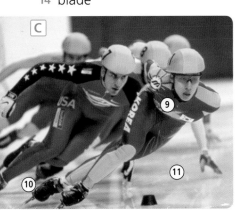

E CROSS-COUNTRY SKIING

15 skier
16 track

F BOBSLEDDING

17 helmet
18 bobsleigh

G SNOWMOBILING

19 snowmobile

Cross-country skiing is slower than downhill skiing.	A Figure skating is more difficult than	Questions for discussion
Bobsledding is more exciting than figure skating.	B .... is .... than	1 Can you do these sports in your country? 2 Which of these sports can be done both indoors and outdoors?

1 lift
2 weights
3 mat
4 run
5 running machine / treadmill
6 exercise bike
7 aerobics
8 rowing machine
9 skip
10 skipping rope
11 throw (a ball)
12 catch (a ball)
13 stretch
14 bend over
15 reach
16 walk
17 hop
18 bounce (a ball)

19 kick (a ball)
20 kneel
21 fall
22 do sit-ups
23 do press-ups
24 do a handstand

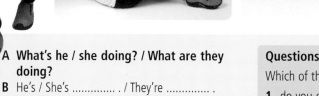

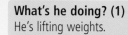

What's he doing? (1)
He's lifting weights.

What are they doing? (7)
They're doing aerobics.

A What's he / she doing? / What are they doing?

B He's / She's .... / They're ....

Questions for discussion
Which of these actions:
1 do you do in tennis?
2 strengthen your legs?

A CLASSICAL CONCERT

1 (symphony) orchestra
2 audience
3 (sheet) music
4 music stand
5 conductor

B BALLET

6 ballerina
7 ballet dancer
8 ballet shoe

C THEATRE

9 spotlight
10 aisle
11 actor

D OPERA

12 stage set
13 chorus
14 singer
15 stage
16 orchestra pit
17 podium

E ROCK CONCERT

18 band
19 singer / vocalist

F CINEMA

20 film, movie *AmE*

When did you last go to the cinema?
I went two days ago.

When did you last go to a classical concert?
I've never been.

A **When did you last go to a / the ....?**
B I went .... ago. / I've never been.

Questions for discussion
1 Do you know any famous singers / actors?
2 What types of films do you like?

HOBBIES

1 coin collecting
2 (coin) album
3 coin
4 stamp collecting
5 (stamp) album
6 magnifying glass
7 photography
8 camera
9 astronomy
10 telescope
11 home improvement / DIY
12 bird-watching
13 binoculars
14 gardening
15 cookery

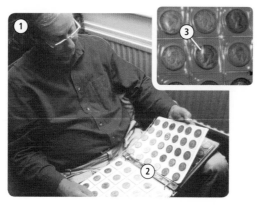
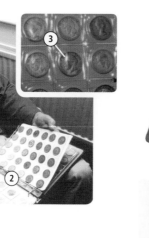

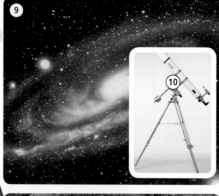

CRAFTS

16 sculpting
17 sculpture
18 embroidery
19 spinning
20 knitting
21 knitting needle
22 sewing machine
23 sewing
24 painting
25 brushes
26 pottery
27 potter's wheel
28 woodworking

GAMES

1 video / computer games
2 Scrabble™
3 chess
4 board
5 pieces
6 dice
7 draughts
8 Monopoly™
9 backgammon
10 cards
11 jigsaw puzzle
12 crossword
13 sudoku

Do you like playing computer games?
Yes, I do. / No, I don't. / I've never tried.

Do you know how to do sudoku puzzles?
Yes, I do. / No, I don't. / I've never tried.

A Do you like playing / doing / solving
..........................?
B Yes, I do. / No, I don't. / I've never tried.

A Do you know how to do / play / solve
..........................?
B ....

Questions for discussion

1 Which of these games can you play online?

2 Which of these games do you think is the most difficult?

95

MUSICAL INSTRUMENTS

STRINGS

1 bow
2 violin
3 viola
4 double bass
5 cello
6 piano

BRASS

7 French horn
8 tuba
9 trumpet
10 trombone

WOODWIND

11 flute
12 piccolo
13 oboe
14 recorder
15 clarinet
16 saxophone
17 bassoon

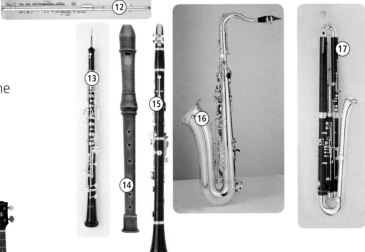

PERCUSSION

18 xylophone
19 drum kit
20 cymbal
21 drum

OTHER INSTRUMENTS

22 accordion
23 harmonica

POP MUSIC

24 mike (microphone)
25 electric guitar
26 bass guitar
27 keyboard
28 amplifier

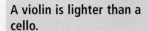

A violin is lighter than a cello.

A double bass is more expensive than a xylophone.

A Drums are louder than ....

A A .... is heavier than a flute.

B A / An .... is .... er / more .... than a / an ....

Questions for discussion

1 Can you play any of these instruments?
2 Which instrument has the nicest sound?
3 Which instruments can be very loud?

1 sea, ocean *AmE*
2 pier
3 deckchair
4 promenade
5 beach towel
6 windbreak
7 shade
8 (beach) umbrella
9 sandcastle
10 sunbather
11 sand
12 life guard
13 bucket, pail *AmE*
14 spade
15 shell
16 bikini
17 swimming costume
18 swimming trunks
19 wave
20 surfer
21 surfboard
22 beach ball
23 Li-lo™ / air bed
24 sunglasses
25 sunscreen

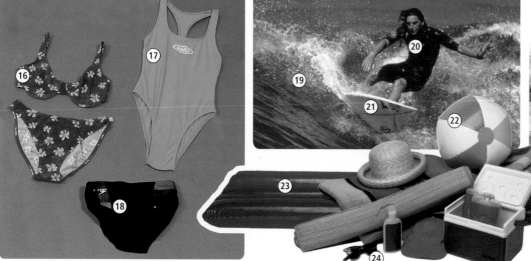

IN THE COUNTRY

A BALLOONING

1 hot-air balloon

B BOATING HOLIDAY

2 barge
3 canal
4 angler
5 fishing rod
6 fishing hook

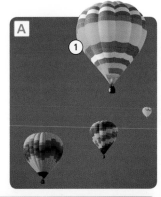

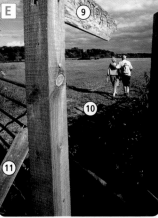

C PONY-TREKKING

D HIKING

7 hiker
8 rucksack

E RAMBLING

9 signpost
10 path
11 stile
12 nature reserve

F CAMPING

13 caravan site
14 campsite
15 picnic
16 camper
17 tent
18 camping stove
19 groundsheet
20 walking boot
21 sleeping bag

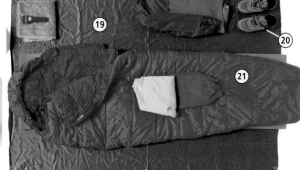

Are you going to go pony-trekking next weekend?
No, I'm not.

Are you going to go rambling next summer?
Yes, I am.

A Are you going to go
.........................ing next summer?
B ....

Questions for discussion

1 What is the difference between hiking and rambling?

2 Which of these activities are popular in your country?

1 theme park
2 roller coaster
3 ride
4 carnival

5 exhibition
6 bookshop
7 museum
8 zoo
9 botanical garden
10 safari park / wildlife park
11 craft fair

12 queue, line *AmE*
13 tour guide
14 tourist
15 church
16 church tower
17 castle

18 village
19 stately home
20 city wall
21 park

Would you rather go to a theme park or a museum?
I'd rather go to a museum.

Neither, I'd rather visit a church.

A Would you rather go to / visit a / an
.... **or a / an** ....?
B I'd rather go to / visit a / an ....

Questions for discussion
1 Which of these places are historical?
2 Are there any of these places near your home?

1 Buckingham Palace
2 Houses of Parliament / Palace of Westminster
3 Big Ben
4 House of Lords
5 House of Commons
6 10 Downing Street
7 Stonehenge
8 Canterbury Cathedral

9 Hampton Court Palace
10 Edinburgh Castle
11 Scottish Parliament

12 Welsh National Assembly
13 Parliament Buildings in Northern Ireland

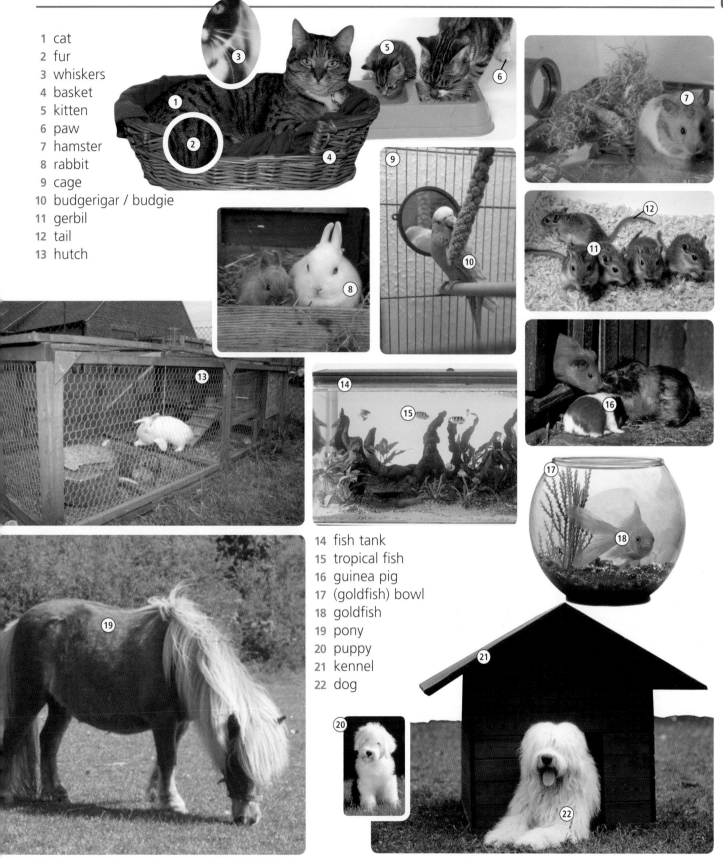

1 cat
2 fur
3 whiskers
4 basket
5 kitten
6 paw
7 hamster
8 rabbit
9 cage
10 budgerigar / budgie
11 gerbil
12 tail
13 hutch

14 fish tank
15 tropical fish
16 guinea pig
17 (goldfish) bowl
18 goldfish
19 pony
20 puppy
21 kennel
22 dog

Have you got any pets?
No, I haven't.
Yes, I have. I've got a dog and some goldfish.

A Have you got any pets?
B ....

Questions for discussion
1 Which of these pets live in a cage or hutch?
2 Which of these pets could you keep in a flat?
3 Which of these pets need to be outdoors?

FARM ANIMALS

1 donkey
2 (nanny) goat
3 kid
4 (billy) goat
5 turkey
6 bull
7 cow
8 calf
9 rabbit
10 sheep
11 lamb
12 goose
13 gosling
14 duck
15 duckling

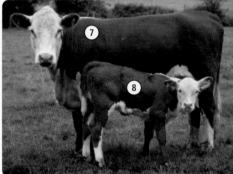

16 chicken
17 cockerel
18 ram
19 horse
20 foal
21 chick
22 pig
23 piglet

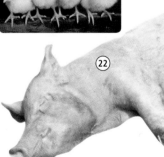

What's a young cow called?
It's called a calf.

What's a young duck called?
It's called a duckling.

A What is a young .... called?
B It's called a ....

Questions for discussion

1 Which of these words only refer to male animals?

2 Which of these animals produce milk for their young?

1 elephant
2 trunk
3 tusk
4 lion
5 mane
6 tiger
7 bear
8 rhinoceros
9 horn
10 hippopotamus
11 kangaroo
12 pouch
13 cheetah
14 buffalo
15 zebra
16 stripes
17 koala bear
18 giraffe
19 leopard
20 spots
21 deer
22 antlers

23 llama
24 gorilla
25 tortoise
26 polar bear
27 fox
28 camel
29 hump
30 monkey
31 lizard
32 frog
33 badger
34 alligator
35 crocodile
36 snake

FISH AND SEA ANIMALS

FISH

1 shark	6 trout
2 tail	7 scales
3 gills	8 angelfish
4 fin	9 eel
5 snout	10 sunfish

SEA ANIMALS

11 whale
12 seal
13 walrus
14 tusk
15 dolphin
16 flipper
17 shrimp
18 crab
19 octopus
20 tentacle
21 clam

22 starfish
23 turtle
24 lobster
25 claw
26 mussels

Which is bigger – a mussel or a turtle?
A turtle.

Which is more friendly – a dolphin or a shark?
A dolphin.

A Which is slower – a shark or a walrus?
B ....
A Which is .... / more .... –
a / an .... or a / an ....?
B ....

Questions for discussion

1 Which of the sea animals can you sometimes find on land?

2 Which of these sea animals are endangered or threatened?

1 flamingo
2 pelican
3 crane
4 robin
5 penguin
6 flipper
7 cockatoo
8 crest
9 owl
10 swallow
11 ostrich
12 eagle
13 beak
14 falcon
15 pheasant
16 tail
17 stork

18 gull
19 hummingbird
20 pigeon
21 nest
22 egg

23 jay
24 peacock
25 feathers
26 parrot
27 swan
28 bill
29 wings
30 crow
31 claws

What do robins look like?
They're small, with brown and red feathers.

What do swans look like?
They're white, with long necks.

A **What do flamingos look like?**
B They're .... with ....

A **What do .... look like?**
B They're .... with ....

Questions for discussion
1 Which of these birds eat meat?
2 Which of these birds can't fly?
3 Which of these birds live in your country?

INSECTS

1 wasps' nest
2 wasp
3 mosquito
4 cockroach
5 beehive
6 moth
7 caterpillar
8 ladybird
9 butterfly
10 dragonfly
11 bee
12 honeycomb
13 grasshopper
14 spider
15 web
16 ant
17 fly

SMALL ANIMALS

18 red squirrel
19 rat
20 mole
21 toad
22 snail
23 hedgehog
24 spines
25 mouse

Do you like all these animals?
Yes, I do. / No, I don't.

Which ones don't you like?
I don't like flies or mice.

A Do you like all these animals?
B ....

A Which ones don't you like?
B ....

Questions for discussion

1 How many different kinds of insects are there?
2 Which of these insects / animals can you sometimes find in the house?

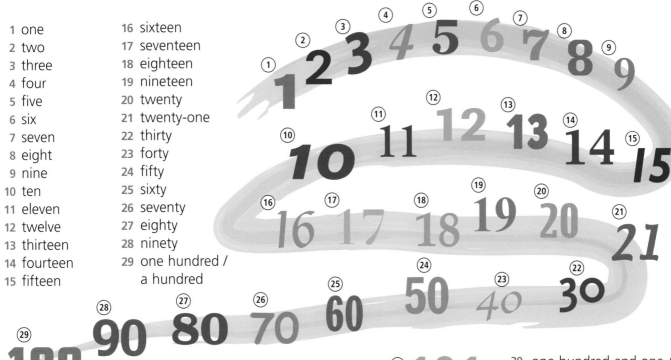

1 one
2 two
3 three
4 four
5 five
6 six
7 seven
8 eight
9 nine
10 ten
11 eleven
12 twelve
13 thirteen
14 fourteen
15 fifteen

16 sixteen
17 seventeen
18 eighteen
19 nineteen
20 twenty
21 twenty-one
22 thirty
23 forty
24 fifty
25 sixty
26 seventy
27 eighty
28 ninety
29 one hundred /
   a hundred

35 plus
36 minus
37 times / multiplied by
38 divided by
39 equals

101
1,000
10,000
100,000
1,000,000

30 one hundred and one /
   a hundred and one
31 one thousand /
   a thousand
32 ten thousand
33 one hundred thousand /
   a hundred thousand
34 one million / a million

40 first
41 second
42 third
43 fourth
44 fifth

45 one hundred percent /
   a hundred percent
46 fifty percent
47 twenty percent
48 ten percent
49 zero / nought / nil

100%   100
        90
        80
        70
        60
50%   50
        40
        30
20%   20
10%   10
        0

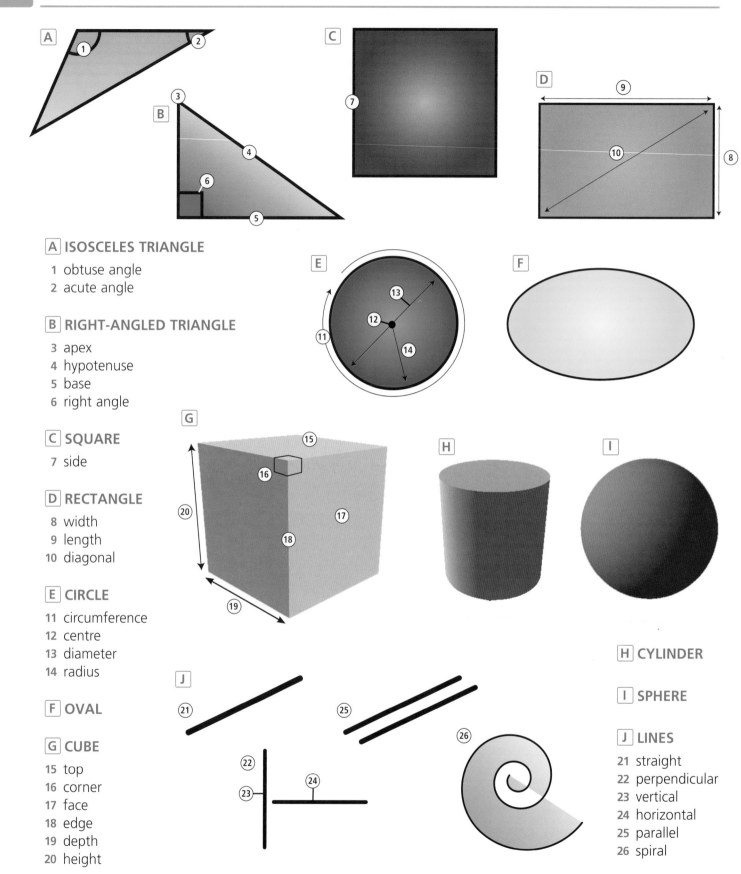

A ISOSCELES TRIANGLE
1 obtuse angle
2 acute angle

B RIGHT-ANGLED TRIANGLE
3 apex
4 hypotenuse
5 base
6 right angle

C SQUARE
7 side

D RECTANGLE
8 width
9 length
10 diagonal

E CIRCLE
11 circumference
12 centre
13 diameter
14 radius

F OVAL

G CUBE
15 top
16 corner
17 face
18 edge
19 depth
20 height

H CYLINDER

I SPHERE

J LINES
21 straight
22 perpendicular
23 vertical
24 horizontal
25 parallel
26 spiral

What's the diameter of the circle? (13)
It's about 3 centimetres.

What's the length of the line? (21)
It's about 3 centimetres.

A What's the .... of the ....?
B It's about .... centimetres.

Questions for discussion
1 Describe an object near you using the words on this page.
2 Give your partner instructions. He / She must draw the shapes that you describe. Give measurements.

A MONTHS

January	February	March	April	May	June
S M T W T F S	S M T W T F S	S M T W T F S	S M T W T F S	S M T W T F S	S M T W T F S

July	August	September	October	November	December

B

B DAYS OF THE WEEK

January

Monday	Tuesday	Wednesday	Thursday	Friday	Saturday	Sunday
	1	2	3	4	5	6
7	8	9	10	11	12	13
14	15	16	17	18	19	20
21	22	23	24	25	26	27
28	29	30	31			

C FESTIVALS

1 New Year's Eve (December 31st)
2 Chinese New Year*
3 St Valentine's Day (February 14th)
4 Mother's Day*
5 Easter Sunday*
6 Father's Day*
7 Halloween (October 31st)
8 Diwali*
9 Bonfire Night / Guy Fawkes' Night (November 5th)
10 Eid ul-Fitr*
11 Remembrance Sunday*
12 Hanukkah*
13 Christmas Eve (December 24th)
14 Christmas Day (December 25th)

* The date changes from year to year.

When's St Valentine's Day?
It's on February the 14th.

When's Bonfire Night?
It's in November.

A When's Christmas Eve?
B ....

A When's ....?
B It's on (date). / It's in (month).

Questions for discussion
1 Which of these are religious festivals?
2 Which festivals do you celebrate in your country? When are they?

1 Christian church
2 vicar
3 Jewish synagogue
4 rabbi
5 Hindu temple
6 Hindu shrine
7 mosque
8 imam
9 Muslim
10 Buddhist temple
11 monk
12 Buddhist shrine
13 Sikh temple
14 Sikh

1 clock
2 hour hand
3 minute hand
4 second hand
5 face
6 (digital) watch
7 (analogue) watch

13 seven fifteen / (a) quarter past seven
14 seven twenty / twenty past seven
15 seven thirty / half past seven
16 seven thirty-five / twenty-five to eight
17 seven forty / twenty to eight
18 seven forty-five / (a) quarter to eight
19 seven fifty / ten to eight
20 seven fifty-five / five to eight
21 eight am / eight (o'clock) in the morning
22 eight pm / eight (o'clock) in the evening

8 twelve o'clock (midnight)
9 twelve o'clock (noon / midday)
10 seven (o'clock)
11 seven oh five / five past seven
12 seven ten / ten past seven

7:00 | 7:05 | 7:10 | 7:15 | 7:20 | 7:30

7:35 | 7:40 | 7:45 | 7:50 | 7:55 | 8:00

Train timetable   Cambridge ⟹ London

MONDAY TO FRIDAY	(23)	(24)	(25)	(26)		(27)	(28)		
Cambridge	10.00	11.00	12.00	13.00	15.00	16.30	18.00	19.30	....	22.30
London	11.30	12.30	13.30	14.45	16.30	18.00	19.30	21.00	.........(30)24.00
SATURDAY									
Cambridge	10.15	11.00	12.15	....	15.00	....	18.15	....	22.15	....
London	11.45	12.30	13.45	....	16.30	.........(29)19.45	....	23.45	....
SUNDAY									
Cambridge	....	11.00	....	13.30	....	17.00	....	20.00	....	22.15
London	....	12.30	....	15.00	....	18.30	....	21.30	....	23.45

23 eleven hundred hours
24 twelve hundred hours
25 thirteen hundred hours
26 fifteen hundred hours
27 eighteen hundred hours
28 nineteen thirty
29 nineteen forty-five
30 twenty-four hundred hours

What time does the first train leave?
It leaves at ten o'clock.

What time does the first train arrive?
It arrives at half past eleven.

A **What time does the ....
train leave / arrive?**
B It leaves / arrives at ....

Questions for discussion
What time do you usually get up / go to bed:
1 on weekdays?
2 at the weekend?
3 during holidays?

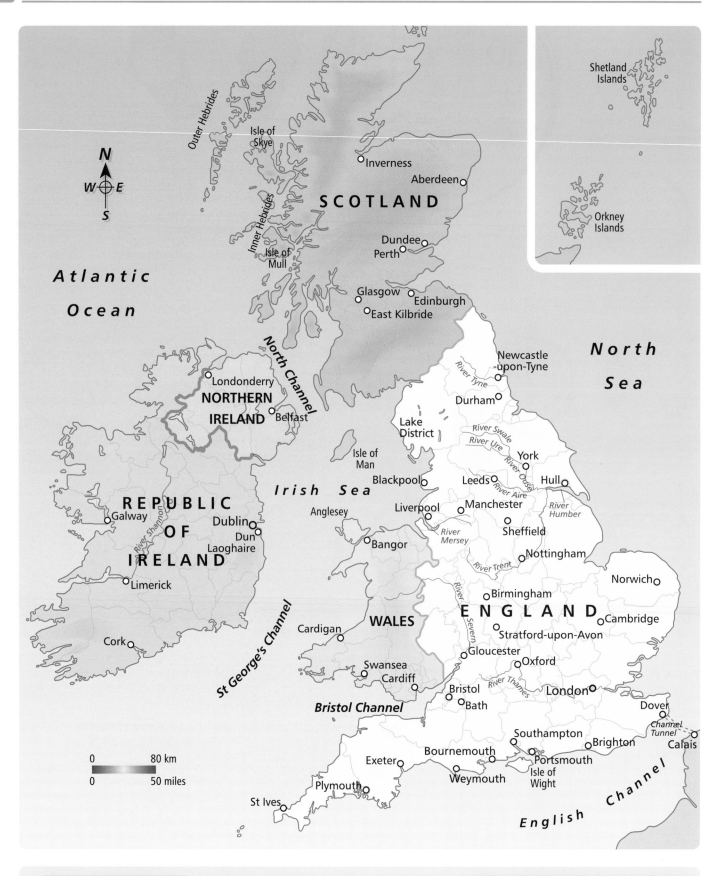

N
W—E
S

Atlantic
Ocean

SCOTLAND

Outer Hebrides
Isle of Skye
Inner Hebrides
Isle of Mull

Inverness
Aberdeen

Dundee
Perth

Glasgow
East Kilbride
Edinburgh

North Channel

Londonderry
NORTHERN
IRELAND
Belfast

Newcastle-upon-Tyne
River Tyne
Durham

North
Sea

REPUBLIC
OF
IRELAND

River Shannon

Galway

Dublin
Dun Laoghaire

Limerick

Cork

Irish Sea

Isle of Man

Blackpool

Anglesey

Bangor

Lake District
River Swale
River Ure
River Ouse
York
Leeds
River Aire
Manchester
Liverpool
River Mersey
Sheffield
River Trent
Nottingham

Hull
River Humber

Norwich

Birmingham
River Severn
ENGLAND
Cambridge
Stratford-upon-Avon

St George's Channel

Cardigan
WALES
Swansea
Cardiff

Gloucester
Oxford
River Thames
Bristol
Bath

London

Dover
Channel Tunnel
Calais

Bristol Channel

Exeter

Plymouth
St Ives

Bournemouth
Weymouth

Southampton
Portsmouth
Isle of Wight

Brighton

English Channel

Shetland Islands

Orkney Islands

0   80 km
0   50 miles

Where's Norwich?
It's in the east of England.

Where's Cardigan?
It's in the west of Wales.

A **Where's Dublin?**
B ....

A **Where's ....?**
B It's in the .... of ....

Questions for discussion
1 Which of these cities are capital cities?
2 Which of these places would you like to visit?

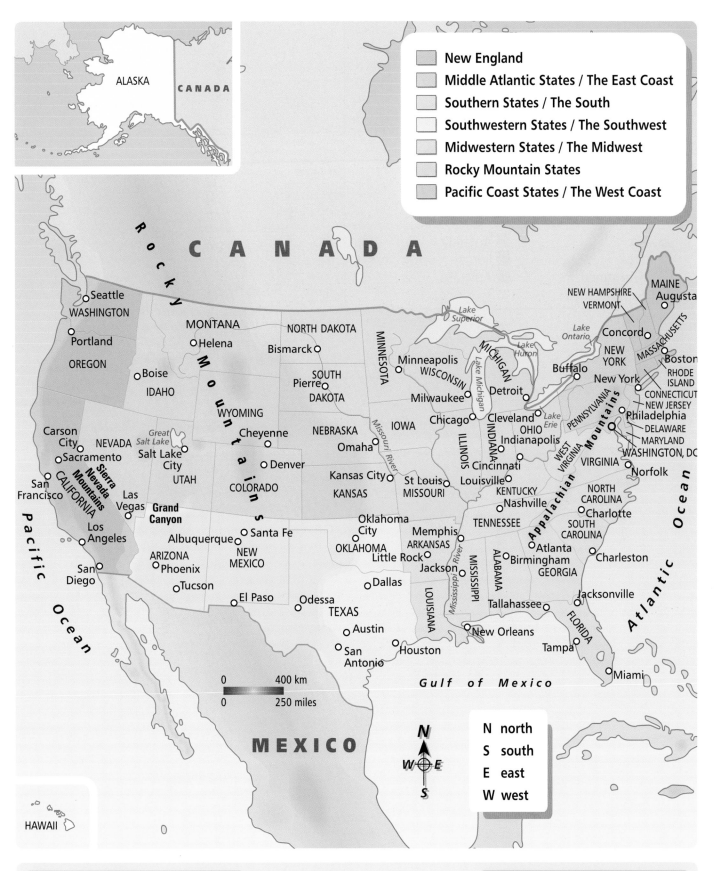

Legend:
- New England
- Middle Atlantic States / The East Coast
- Southern States / The South
- Southwestern States / The Southwest
- Midwestern States / The Midwest
- Rocky Mountain States
- Pacific Coast States / The West Coast

ALASKA — CANADA

CANADA

Rocky Mountains

Seattle — WASHINGTON
Portland — OREGON
Boise — IDAHO
Helena — MONTANA
Bismarck — NORTH DAKOTA
Pierre — SOUTH DAKOTA
MINNESOTA
Minneapolis — WISCONSIN
Milwaukee
Cheyenne — WYOMING
NEBRASKA — Omaha
IOWA
Chicago — ILLINOIS
MICHIGAN
Detroit
Cleveland — OHIO
INDIANA — Indianapolis
Lake Superior
Lake Huron
Lake Michigan
Lake Ontario
Lake Erie
Buffalo
New York — NEW YORK
NEW HAMPSHIRE
VERMONT
MAINE — Augusta
Concord
MASSACHUSETTS — Boston
RHODE ISLAND
CONNECTICUT
NEW JERSEY
PENNSYLVANIA — Philadelphia
DELAWARE
MARYLAND
WASHINGTON, DC
WEST VIRGINIA
VIRGINIA
Norfolk

Carson City — NEVADA
Sacramento
Great Salt Lake
Salt Lake City — UTAH
San Francisco — CALIFORNIA
Sierra Nevada Mountains
Las Vegas
Grand Canyon
Los Angeles
San Diego
Denver — COLORADO
Kansas City
KANSAS
St Louis — MISSOURI
Cincinnati
Louisville — KENTUCKY
Nashville — TENNESSEE
Appalachian Mountains
NORTH CAROLINA — Charlotte
SOUTH CAROLINA
Atlanta
Charleston

Albuquerque — NEW MEXICO
Santa Fe
ARIZONA — Phoenix
Tucson
El Paso
Odessa
TEXAS
Oklahoma City — OKLAHOMA
Little Rock — ARKANSAS
Memphis
Dallas
Jackson — MISSISSIPPI
ALABAMA — Birmingham
GEORGIA
Jacksonville
Tallahassee — FLORIDA
Tampa
Miami
LOUISIANA
New Orleans
Houston
San Antonio
Austin

Mississippi River
Missouri River

Pacific Ocean
Atlantic Ocean
Gulf of Mexico

MEXICO

HAWAII

0 — 400 km
0 — 250 miles

N north
S south
E east
W west

Where's Nebraska?
It's east of Wyoming and west of Iowa.

Where's Oklahoma?
It's south of Kansas and north of Texas.

A Where's Indiana?
B ....

A Where's ....?
B It's .... of ....
and .... of ....

Questions for discussion
1 Which of the states have a sea coast?
2 Which of the states are on a lake?
3 Which of the states have a border with another country?

Continents

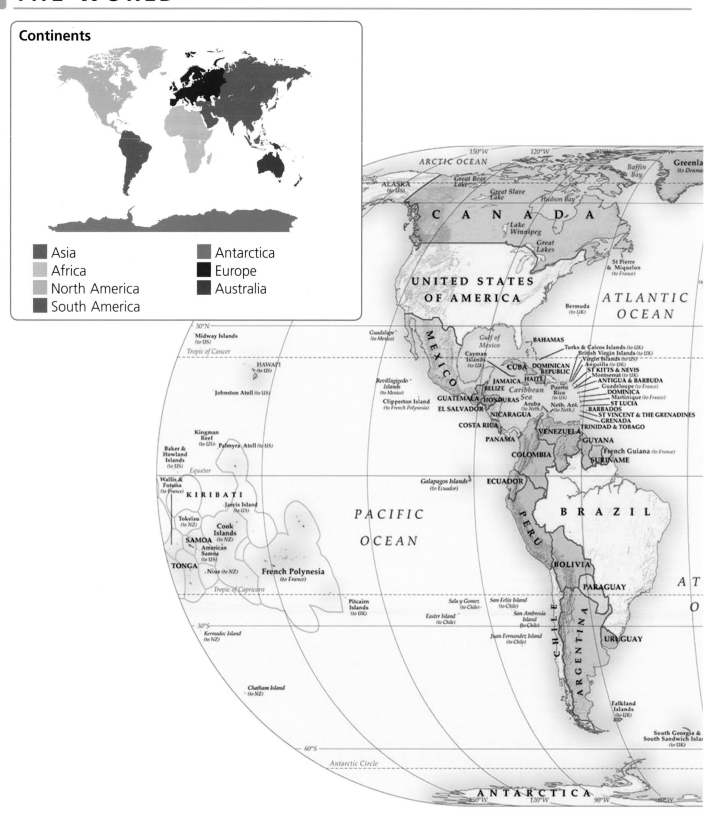

Asia
Africa
North America
South America
Antarctica
Europe
Australia

Which continent is the United Kingdom located on?
The United Kingdom is in Europe.

A Which continent is Mexico located on?
B Mexico is in ....

A Which continent is .... located on?
B .... is in ....

Questions for discussion
1 Which is the largest continent in the world?
2 Which is the smallest continent?
3 What are the ten biggest countries by area?

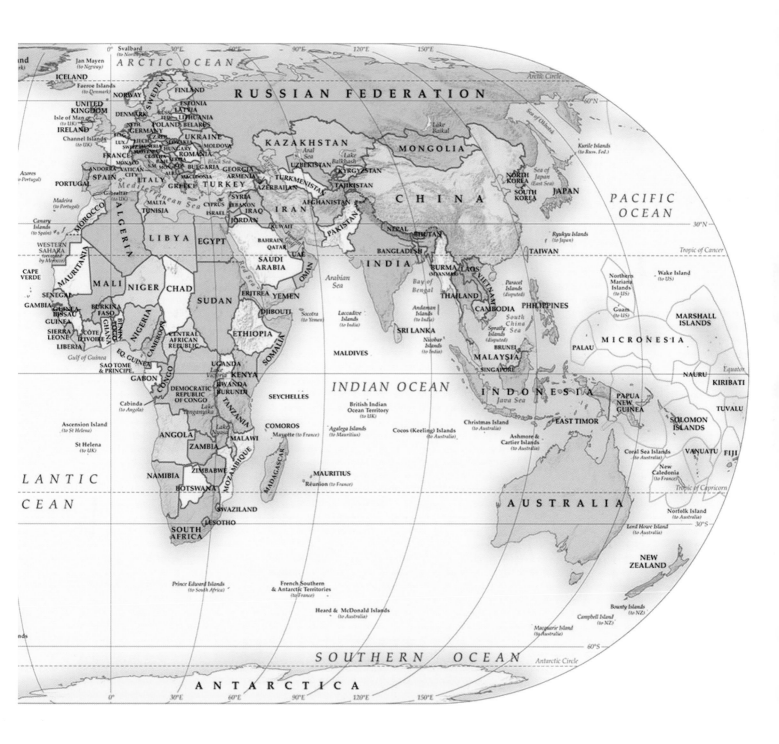

Warsaw is the capital of Poland.

Poland is a member state of the European Union.

A Lisbon is the capital of ....

B .... is a member state of the ....

A .... **is the capital of** ....

B .... is (not) a member state of the
.... (Refer to p. 116.)

Questions for discussion

1 Which country do you come from?

2 What's the capital city?

3 Which countries have you been to?

4 Which countries would you like to visit?

Current member states of the European Union (EU)

Austria	Estonia	Italy	Portugal
Belgium	Finland	Latvia	Romania
Bulgaria	France	Lithuania	Slovakia
Croatia	Germany	Luxembourg	Slovenia
Cyprus	Greece	Malta	Spain
Czech Republic	Hungary	Netherlands	Sweden
Denmark	Ireland	Poland	United Kingdom

1 peak
2 mountain
3 lake
4 cactus
5 meadow
6 hill
7 valley
8 acorn
9 oak tree
10 palm tree
11 desert
12 (sand) dune
13 reservoir
14 dam
15 fir tree
16 fir cone
17 forest
18 island
19 coastline
20 pond
21 wood
22 waterfall
23 stream / brook

24 rock
25 cliff
26 grass
27 canal
28 cave
29 beach
30 river
31 field
32 chestnut tree
33 conkers

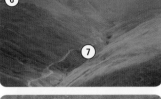

Is there a mountain near your home?
Yes, there is.

Are there any woods near your home?
No, there aren't.

A **Is there a / Are there any** .... **near** ....?

B Yes, there is. / No, there isn't. / Yes, there are. / No, there aren't.

Questions for discussion
What's the difference between:
1 a hill and a mountain?
2 a river and a lake?
3 a waterfall and a stream?

SEASONS
1 summer
2 autumn,
fall AmE
3 winter
4 spring

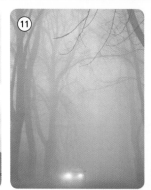

WEATHER
5 rainy
6 sunny
7 snowy
8 icy
9 clear
10 cloudy / overcast
11 foggy
12 hazy

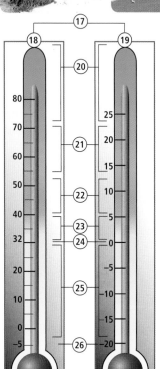

13 windy
14 stormy
15 thunder and lightning
16 rainbow

TEMPERATURE
17 thermometer
18 degrees Fahrenheit
19 degrees Celsius / degrees Centigrade
20 hot
21 warm
22 cool / chilly
23 cold
24 freezing
25 below freezing
26 five (degrees) below (zero) / minus
twenty degrees

What's the weather like?
It's warm and sunny.

What do you need when it's freezing?
You need warm clothes, gloves and boots.

A **What's the weather like? (13) (22)**
B It's .... and ....

A **What do you need when it's ....?**
B You need ....

Questions for discussion
1 How many seasons are there
in your country? What's the
weather like in each season?
2 Which is your favourite season?

THE PLANETS

1 Mercury
2 Venus
3 Earth
4 Mars
5 Jupiter
6 Saturn
7 Uranus
8 Neptune
9 Pluto

10 sun
11 solar system

12 orbit
13 star
14 constellation
15 comet
16 satellite
17 galaxy
18 new moon
19 half moon
20 full moon
21 moon

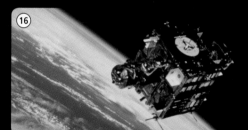

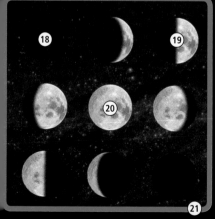

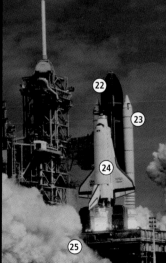

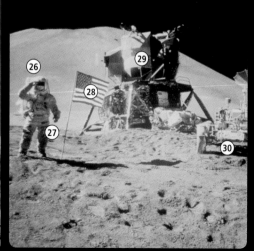

22 fuel tank
23 booster r
24 space sh
25 launch p
26 astronau
27 space sui
28 flag
29 lunar mo
30 lunar veh

Which planet is the smallest?
Mercury.

Which planet is the most distant from the Sun?
Pluto.

A Which planet is the nearest to Earth?
B ....

A Which planet is the .... est / the most ....?
B ....

Questions for discussion
1 Do you know any constellations?
2 Have you ever seen a comet?
3 Which planets has man explored?

COMPUTERS AND SOFTWARE

A HARDWARE

1 scanner
2 personal computer / PC
3 monitor
4 web-cam
5 display screen
6 CD-ROM drive
7 hard disk drive
8 printer
9 keyboard
10 mouse mat
11 mouse
12 laptop
13 external hard drive
14 speakers
15 Memory Stick™
16 dongle
17 CD-ROM
18 console
19 gamepad
20 joystick
21 electronic /
   computer game

B SOFTWARE

22 word processor
23 menu bar
24 toolbar
25 document
26 spreadsheet
27 table
28 folder

29 file
30 cursor
31 font
32 window
33 icon

What's a dongle used for?
It's used for running protected software and for wireless Internet access.

What's a joystick used for?
It's used for controlling video games.

A What's a CD-ROM used for?
B It's used for ....

A What's a .... used for?
B It's used for ....

Questions for discussion
1 How much time do you spend in front of a computer each day?
2 What software are you familiar with?

THE WORLD WIDE WEB

1 web browser
2 Internet service provider
3 password
4 Internet café
5 keyword
6 search engine
7 search page
8 hyperlink
9 website
10 web address (URL)
11 home page

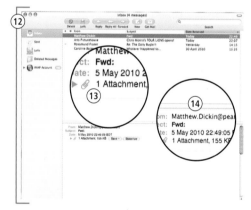

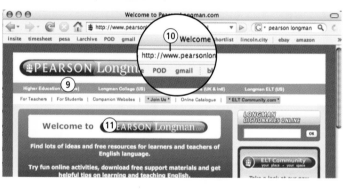

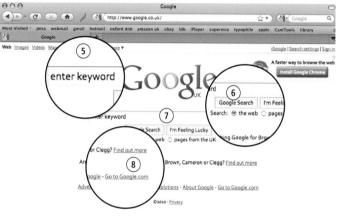

E-MAIL

12 e-mail software
13 file attachment
14 e-mail address
15 network
16 server

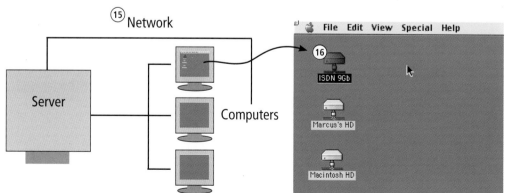

You have to use a search engine if you want to find information on the Internet.

You have to know your user name and password if you want to sign in.

A You have to .... if you want to ....

Questions for discussion

1 How often do you use the Internet?
2 What do you use it for?
3 Do you ever have any problems?

1 clock-radio
2 Blue-ray™ player
3 DVD player
4 DVD / digital versatile disc
5 satellite TV / cable TV
6 digi-box
7 remote control
8 flatscreen TV
9 games console
10 control pad
11 tuner
12 MP3 player
13 speaker
14 compact disc / CD player
15 personal computer / PC
16 headphones
17 e-reader
18 palmtop
19 digital radio

1 (cordless) phone
2 keypad
3 base
4 answering machine
5 charger
6 mobile, cell phone *AmE*
7 Bluetooth™ headset
8 text message
9 pager

10 electronic personal organiser / PDA
11 pocket calculator
12 flash
13 film
14 lens
15 (still) camera
16 tripod
17 digital camera
18 digital SLR camera
19 camcorder
20 slide projector
21 slides
22 memory card
23 sat-nav
24 torch
25 battery
26 light bulb

What can you do with your PDA?
I can transfer documents, view images, take photos, shoot short videos, browse the Internet and check my e-mail.

A What can you do with your mobile phone?
B I can make ...., send ...., take ...., play .... and search the ....

A What can you do with your ....?
B I can ....

Questions for discussion

1 How often do you buy a new mobile phone?

2 Which of these things: do you have? would you like to have?

ADJECTIVES 1

FEELINGS

1 miserable
2 sad
3 pleased
4 happy
5 ecstatic
6 annoyed
7 angry
8 furious
9 nervous
10 suspicious
11 scared / afraid
12 shy
13 surprised
14 confused
15 bored

Is she sad? (2)
Yes, she is.

Does he look bored? (11)
No, he doesn't. He looks scared.

A Is he / she ....?
B Yes, he / she is. / No, he / she isn't.

A Does he / she look ....?
B Yes, he / she does. / No, he / she doesn't.

Questions for discussion

1 How do you usually feel when you finish exams?
2 How would you feel if you forgot your girlfriend's / boyfriend's / spouse's birthday?

OPPOSITES

1 neat / tidy
2 messy / untidy

3 dry
4 wet

5 tight
6 loose

7 heavy
8 light

9 open
10 closed

11 short
12 long

13 empty
14 full

15 rough
16 smooth

17 near / close
18 far

19 dark
20 light

21 thin
22 thick

23 narrow
24 wide

25 hard
26 soft

£1.05 (27)

£150.00 (28)

27 cheap
28 expensive

29 deep
30 shallow

31 fast
32 slow

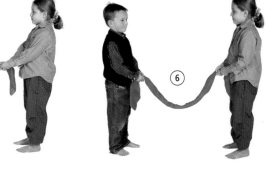

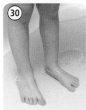

Is it short? (11)
Yes, it is.

Is it expensive? (27)
No, it isn't. It's cheap.

A **Is it narrow? (24)**
B ....

A **Is it** ....?
B Yes, it is. / No, it isn't. It's ....

Questions for discussion

Use as many of these adjectives as possible to describe the following:

1 an item of clothing you are wearing.

2 an object near you.

PREPOSITIONS 1

1 from
2 to

3 in front of
4 behind

5 over
6 under

7 in
8 out

9 up
10 down

11 onto
12 off

13 on
14 off

15 above
16 below

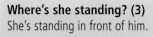

Where's she standing? (3)
She's standing in front of him.

Where's she sitting? (16)
She's sitting below the boy.

A Where is he / she / it
standing / sitting / going?

B He's / She's / It's
standing / sitting / going
....

Questions for discussion

1 Describe your position in the room using as many of these prepositions as possible.

2 The prepositions 'on' and 'off' are used in phrasal verbs such as 'switch on' and 'switch off'. Can you think of other examples?

1 round
2 between
3 against
4 across
5 away from
6 towards
7 outside
8 inside
9 into
10 through
11 out of

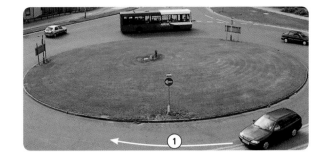

12 along
13 beside / next to
14 at the top
15 in the middle
16 at the bottom
17 on top of
18 under / underneath

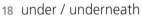

Where is the table? (2)
It's between the boy and the girl.

What's he doing? (4)
He's walking across the street.

A What's / What are he / she / they doing?

B He's / She's / They're
....

Questions for discussion

1 Describe the location of the objects around you using as many of these prepositions as possible.

2 Look outside and describe any people or objects that are moving.

PRONUNCIATION TABLE

All the words in the *Longman Photo Dictionary* are pronounced on the CDs.
This Pronunciation table shows you how to say the words in the Word list.

Symbol Consonants	Keyword	Symbol Vowels	Keyword
p	**p**ack	e	b**e**d
b	**b**ack	æ	b**a**d
t	**t**ie	i	happ**y**
d	**d**ie	iː	k**ee**per
k	**c**lass	ɪ	b**i**d
g	**g**lass	ɑː	f**a**ther
tʃ	**ch**urch	ɔː	c**a**ller
dʒ	**j**udge	ɒ	p**o**t
f	**f**ew	ʊ	p**u**t
v	**v**iew	uː	b**oo**t
θ	**th**row	u	grad**u**al
ð	**th**ough	ʌ	c**u**t
s	**s**oon	ɜː	b**i**rd
z	**z**oo	ə	b**a**nana
ʃ	**sh**oe	eɪ	m**a**ke
ʒ	mea**s**ure	aɪ	b**i**te
m	su**m**	ɔɪ	b**oy**
n	su**n**	aʊ	n**ow**
ŋ	su**ng**	əʊ	b**oa**t
h	**h**ot	ɪə	h**ere**
l	**l**ot	eə	h**air**
r	**r**od	ʊə	t**our**
j	**y**et	eɪə	pl**ayer**
w	**w**et	aɪə	t**ire**
		ɔɪə	empl**oyer**
		aʊə	fl**ower**
		əʊə	l**ower**

/'/ shows main stress

/ˌ/ shows secondary stress

/ʳ/ means the /r/ sound is pronounced in American English but is usually not pronounced in British English, except at the end of a word when the word that follows begins with a vowel sound

/ə/ means that /ə/ may or may not be used

128

WORD LIST

blackboard /ˈblækbɔːd/ 56
blackcurrant /ˌblækˈkʌrənt/ 61
blade /bleɪd/ 91
blanket /ˈblæŋkɪt/ 13
blender /ˈblendəʳ/ 11
blini /ˈbliːni/ 65
blond hair /ˌblɒnd ˈheəʳ/ 36
blood /blʌd/ 41
blood pressure gauge /ˈblʌd preʃə ˌgeɪdʒ/ 43
blouse /blaʊz‖blaʊs/ 47
blow-dry /ˈbləʊ draɪ/ 39
blue /bluː/ 51
blue cheese /ˌ. ˈ./ 64
blue collar worker /ˌ. ˈ.. ˌ../ 25
blueberry /ˈbluːbəri/ 61
Blue-ray™ player /ˈbluː reɪ ˌpleɪəʳ/ 122
Bluetooth™ headset /ˌbluːtuːθ ˈhedset/ 123
blusher /ˈblʌʃəʳ/ 40
board /bɔːd/ 95
boarding pass /ˈbɔːdɪŋ pɑːs/ 76
boarding school /ˈbɔːdɪŋ skuːl/ 54
boating /ˈbəʊtɪŋ/ 98
bobsledding /ˈbɒbsledɪŋ/ 91
bobsleigh /ˈbɒbsleɪ/ 91
boil /bɔɪl/ 69
boiled egg /ˌbɔɪld ˈeg/ 70
bollard /ˈbɒləd, -lɑːd/ 80
bolt /bəʊlt/ 29
Bonfire Night /ˈbɒnfaɪə naɪt/ 109
bonnet /ˈbɒnɪt/ 73
book /bʊk/ 55
book of stamps /ˌbʊk əv ˈstæmps/ 82, 83
bookcase /ˈbʊk-keɪs/ 14
books /bʊks/ 14
bookshop /ˈbʊkʃɒp/ 84, 99
booster rocket /ˈbuːstə ˌrɒkɪt/ 119
boot /buːt/ 73
boots /buːts/ 47
border /ˈbɔːdəʳ/ 18
bored /bɔːd/ 124
borscht /bɔːʃt/ 65
botanical garden /bəˌtænɪkəl ˈgɑːdn/ 99
bottle /ˈbɒtl/ 68
bottle opener /ˈbɒtl ˌəʊpənəʳ/ 11
bottled food /ˈbɒtld ˌfuːd/ 62
bounce a ball /ˌbaʊns ə ˈbɔːl/ 92
bouncer /ˈbaʊnsəʳ/ 16
boundary /ˈbaʊndəri/ 86
bow /baʊ/ 78, 89, 96
bow tie /ˌbəʊ ˈtaɪ/ 48
bowl /bəʊl/ 15
bowler /ˈbəʊləʳ/ 86
box /bɒks/ 68
box of chocolates /ˌbɒks əv ˈtʃɒklɪts/ 83
box of tissues /ˌ. . ˈ../ 16
boxer /ˈbɒksəʳ/ 87
boxer shorts /ˈ.. ˌ./ 48
boxing /ˈbɒksɪŋ/ 87
boy /bɔɪ/ 6
bra /brɑː/ 47

brace /breɪs/ 45
bracelet /ˈbreɪslɪt/ 53
braces /ˈbreɪsɪz/ 53
bradawl /ˈbrædɔːl/ 29
braiding /ˈbreɪdɪŋ/ 39
braids /breɪdz/ 36
brain /breɪn/ 35
brake /breɪk/ 73
brake light /ˈ. ./ 73
brass /brɑːs/ 96
Brazil nut /brəˈzɪl nʌt/ 61
bread /bred/ 70
break /breɪk/ 38, 69
breakfast /ˈbrekfəst/ 70
breastbone /ˈbrestbəʊn/ 35
brick /brɪk/ 31
bricklayer /ˈbrɪkˌleɪəʳ/ 23
bridge /brɪdʒ/ 74, 81
brie /briː/ 64
briefcase /ˈbriːfkeɪs/ 53
Brighton /ˈbraɪtn/ 112
Bristol /ˈbrɪstəl/ 112
broad bean /brɔːd ˈbiːn/ 60
broccoli /ˈbrɒkəli/ 59
broken leg /ˌbrəʊkən ˈleg/ 41
broken zip /ˌbrəʊkən ˈzɪp/ 52
brooch /brəʊtʃ/ 53
brook /brʊk/ 117
broom /bruːm/ 17
brother /ˈbrʌðəʳ/ 7
brothers-in-law /ˈbrʌðəz ɪn lɔː/ 7
brown /braʊn/ 51
brown hair /ˌ. ˈ./ 36
bruise /bruːz/ 41
brush /brʌʃ/ 17, 40
brush your hair /ˌ. . ˈ./ 8
brush your teeth /ˌbrʌʃ jɔː ˈtiːθ/ 8
brushes /ˈbrʌʃɪz/ 94
Brussels sprouts /ˌbrʌsəlz ˈspraʊts/ 59
bucket /ˈbʌkɪt/ 17, 97
Buckingham Palace /ˌbʌkɪŋəm ˈpælɪs/ 100
buckle /ˈbʌkəl/ 50, 53
Buddhist shrine /ˌbʊdɪst ˈʃraɪn/ 110
Buddhist temple /ˌbʊdɪst ˈtempəl/ 110
budgerigar /ˈbʌdʒərɪgɑːʳ/ 101
budgie /ˈbʌdʒi/ 101
buffalo /ˈbʌfələʊ/ 103
buggy /ˈbʌgi/ 16
building blocks /ˈbɪldɪŋ blɒks/ 55
Bulgaria /bʌlˈgeəriə/ 116
bull /bʊl/ 102
bulldozer /ˈbʊldəʊzəʳ/ 31
bumper /ˈbʌmpəʳ/ 73
bungalow /ˈbʌŋgələʊ/ 9
bunsen burner /ˌbʌnsən ˈbɜːnəʳ/ 56
burgers /ˈbɜːgəz/ 62
bus /bʌs/ 71, 74, 80
bus driver /ˈbʌs ˌdraɪvəʳ/ 26, 71
bus lane /ˈbʌs leɪn/ 80
bus shelter /ˈbʌs ˌʃeltəʳ/ 80
bus stop /ˈbʌs stɒp/ 71, 80
bush /bʊʃ/ 18

business studies /ˈbɪznəs ˌstʌdiz/ 57
butcher /ˈbʊtʃəʳ/ 23
butter /ˈbʌtəʳ/ 62, 70
butterfly /ˈbʌtəflaɪ/ 106
butternut squash /ˌbʌtənʌt ˈskwɒʃ/ 60
buttocks /ˈbʌtəks/ 34
button /ˈbʌtn/ 50
buttonhole /ˈbʌtnhəʊl/ 50
cabbage /ˈkæbɪdʒ/ 59
cabin /ˈkæbɪn/ 77, 78
cabin cruiser /ˈkæbɪn ˌkruːzəʳ/ 78
cable /ˈkeɪbəl/ 78
cable TV /ˌkeɪbəl tiː ˈviː/ 122
cactus /ˈkæktəs/ 117
cafeteria /ˌkæfəˈtɪəriə/ 58
cafetière /ˌkæfəˈtjeəʳ/ 10
cage /keɪdʒ/ 101
cagoule /kəˈguːl/ 46
cake /keɪk/ 64
cake stand /ˈkeɪk stænd/ 15
cake tin /ˈkeɪk tɪn/ 11
calculator /ˈkælkjʊleɪtəʳ/ 56
calendar /ˈkælɪndəʳ/ 27
calf /kɑːf‖kæf/ 34, 102
California /ˌkælɪˈfɔːnjə/ 113
call centre operator /ˈkɔːl sentə ˌɒpəreɪtəʳ/ 25
calling from a public phone box /ˌkɔːlɪŋ frəm ə ˌpʌblɪk ˈfəʊn bɒks/ 85
Cambridge /ˈkeɪmbrɪdʒ/ 112
camcorder /ˈkæmˌkɔːdəʳ/ 123
camel /ˈkæməl/ 51, 103
camera /ˈkæmərə/ 94
camisole /ˈkæmɪsəʊl/ 47
camper /ˈkæmpəʳ/ 98
camping /ˈkæmpɪŋ/ 98
camping stove /ˈkæmpɪŋ stəʊv/ 98
campsite /ˈkæmpsaɪt/ 98
campus /ˈkæmpəs/ 58
can /kæn/ 68
canal /kəˈnæl/ 98, 117
candle /ˈkændl/ 15
candy AmE /ˈkændi/ 67
canoe /kəˈnuː/ 90
canoeing /kəˈnuːɪŋ/ 90
canoeist /kəˈnuːɪst/ 90
Canterbury Cathedral /ˌkæntəbəri kəˈθiːdrəl/ 100
captain /ˈkæptɪn/ 77
car /kɑːʳ/ 74
car seat /ˈkɑː siːt/ 16
caravan /ˈkærəvæn/ 72
caravan site /ˈkærəvæn saɪt/ 98
card shop /ˈkɑːd ʃɒp/ 84
Cardiff /ˈkɑːdɪf/ 112
cardigan /ˈkɑːdɪgən/ 46
Cardigan /ˈkɑːdɪgən/ 112
cardiologist /ˌkɑːdiˈɒlədʒɪst/ 43
cards /kɑːdz/ 95
care worker /ˈkeə ˌwɜːkəʳ/ 26
cargo /ˈkɑːgəʊ/ 78
carnival /ˈkɑːnɪvəl/ 99
carpenter /ˈkɑːpɪntəʳ/ 23
carpet /ˈkɑːpɪt/ 13
carriage /ˈkærɪdʒ/ 71

carrier bag /ˈkæriə bæg/ 62
carrot /ˈkærət/ 59
carrots /ˈkærəts/ 66
carry /ˈkæri/ 37
cars /kɑːz/ 72
carton /ˈkɑːtn/ 68
cash /kæʃ/ 79
cash machine /ˈkæʃ məˌʃiːn/ 84
cashew nut /ˈkæʃuː nʌt‖kəˈʃuː nʌt/ 61
cashier /kæˈʃɪəʳ/ 25, 62, 79
cashpoint /ˈkæʃpɔɪnt/ 79
cashpoint card /ˈ.. ˌ./ 79
casserole dish /ˈkæsərəʊl dɪʃ/ 11
cassette player /kəˈset ˌpleɪəʳ/ 73
castle /ˈkɑːsəl/ 99
casual wear /ˈkæʒuəl weəʳ/ 48
cat /kæt/ 101
cat food /ˈkæt fuːd/ 63
cat's eyes /ˈ. ./ 74
catch a ball /ˌkætʃ ə ˈbɔːl/ 92
caterpillar /ˈkætəˌpɪləʳ/ 106
cauliflower /ˈkɒlɪˌflaʊəʳ/ 59
cave /keɪv/ 117
CCTV camera /ˌsiː siː tiː viː ˈkæmərə/ 80
CD player /ˌsiː ˈdiː ˌpleɪəʳ/ 56, 73
CD-ROM /ˌsiː diː ˈrɒm/ 120
CD-ROM drive /ˌsiː diː ˈrɒm draɪv/ 120
ceiling /ˈsiːlɪŋ/ 20
celeriac /səˈleəriæk/ 60
celery /ˈseləri/ 59
cell phone AmE /ˈsel fəʊn/ 123
cellar /ˈseləʳ/ 20
cello /ˈtʃeləʊ/ 96
cement /sɪˈment/ 31
cement mixer /sɪˈment ˌmɪksəʳ/ 31
centimetre /ˈsentɪmiːtəʳ/ 68
central reservation /ˌsentrəl rezəˈveɪʃən/ 74
centre /ˈsentəʳ/ 108
centre circle /ˌ.. ˈ../ 86
cereal /ˈsɪəriəl/ 63, 70
chain /tʃeɪn/ 53
chair /tʃeəʳ/ 15
chairlift /ˈtʃeəlɪft/ 91
chalk /tʃɔːk/ 56
chambermaid /ˈtʃeɪmbəˌmeɪd/ 32
champagne /ʃæmˈpeɪn/ 66
changing mat /ˈtʃeɪndʒɪŋ mæt/ 16
charger /ˈtʃɑːdʒəʳ/ 123
cheap /tʃiːp/ 125
checked /tʃekt/ 51
check-in desk /ˈtʃek ɪn desk/ 76
checking in /ˌtʃekɪŋ ˈɪn/ 32
checking out /ˌtʃekɪŋ ˈaʊt/ 32
checkout area /ˈtʃekaʊt ˌeəriə/ 62
checkout desk /ˈtʃek-aʊt ˌdesk/ 62
cheek /tʃiːk/ 35
cheese /tʃiːz/ 62
cheese on toast /ˌ. . ˈ./ 70

cheeseburger /'tʃiːzbɜːgəʳ/ **67**
cheesecake /'tʃiːzkeɪk/ **66**
cheetah /'tʃiːtə/ **103**
chef /ʃef/ **23**
chemist's /'kemɪsts/ **84**
chemistry /'kemɪstri/ **57**
cheque /tʃek/ **79**
cheque card /'tʃek kɑːd/ **79**
chequebook /'tʃekbʊk/ **79**
cherry /'tʃeri/ **61**
chess /tʃes/ **95**
chest /tʃest/ **34**
chest of drawers /ˌ. . ˈ./ **13**
chestnut tree /'tʃesnʌt triː/ **117**
chewing gum /'tʃuːɪŋ gʌm/ **83**
Chicago /ʃɪˈkɑːgəʊ/ **113**
chick /tʃɪk/ **102**
chicken /'tʃɪkɪn/ **102**
chicken leg /'tʃɪkɪn leg/ **64**
chicken liver pâté /ˌtʃɪkɪn ˌlɪvə ˈpæteɪ/ **65**
chicken tikka masala /ˌtʃɪkɪn ˌtiːkə məˈsɑːlə/ **65**
chicken wrap /ˌtʃɪkɪn ˈræp/ **67**
child /tʃaɪld/ **6**
childminder /'tʃaɪldˌmaɪndəʳ/ **26**
children /'tʃɪldrən/ **7**
chilli pepper /'tʃɪli pepəʳ/ **59**
chilly /'tʃɪli/ **118**
chimney /'tʃɪmni/ **9**
chin /tʃɪn/ **34**
Chinese New Year /ˌtʃaɪniːz njuː ˈjɪəʳ/ **109**
chips /tʃɪps/ **62, 67, 70**
chips *AmE* /tʃɪps/ **67**
chiropodist /kɪˈrɒpədɪst/ **43**
chisel /'tʃɪzəl/ **29**
chives /tʃaɪvz/ **60**
chocolate gateau /ˌtʃɒklɪt ˈgætəʊ/ **66**
chop /tʃɒp/ **69**
chopped tomatoes /ˌtʃɒpt təˈmɑːtəʊz‖-ˈmeɪ-/ **62**
chopping board /'tʃɒpɪŋ bɔːd/ **11**
chorizo /tʃəˈriːzəʊ/ **64**
chorus /'kɔːrəs/ **93**
Christian church /ˌkrɪstʃən ˈtʃɜːtʃ/ **110**
Christmas Day /ˌkrɪsməs ˈdeɪ/ **109**
Christmas Eve /ˌkrɪsməs ˈiːv/ **109**
chrysanthemum /krɪˈsænθɪməm/ **18**
church /tʃɜːtʃ/ **99**
church tower /ˌtʃɜːtʃ ˈtaʊəʳ/ **99**
cinema /'sɪnɪmə/ **93**
circle /'sɜːkəl/ **108**
circumference /səˈkʌmfərəns/ **108**
Citizens Advice Bureau /ˌsɪtɪzənz ədˈvaɪs bjʊəˌrəʊ/ **22**
city wall /ˌsɪti ˈwɔːl/ **99**
clam /klæm/ **104**
clap /klæp/ **37**
clarinet /ˌklærɪˈnet/ **96**
classical concert /ˌklæsɪkəl ˈkɒnsət/ **93**
classroom /'klɑːsrʊm/ **56**

claw /klɔː/ **104**
claws /klɔːz/ **105**
cleaner /'kliːnəʳ/ **26**
cleaning fluid /'kliːnɪŋ ˌfluːɪd/ **45**
clear /klɪəʳ/ **118**
clementine /'kleməntiːn/ **61**
cliff /klɪf/ **117**
climber /'klaɪməʳ/ **89**
climbing /'klaɪmɪŋ/ **89**
climbing frame /'klaɪmɪŋ freɪm/ **55**
clingfilm™ /'klɪŋfɪlm/ **10**
clock /klɒk/ **71, 111**
clock-radio /ˌklɒk ˈreɪdiəʊ/ **122**
close /kləʊs/ **125**
closed /kləʊzd/ **125**
clothesline /'kləʊzlaɪn/ **17**
cloudy /'klaʊdi/ **118**
clutch /klʌtʃ/ **73**
clutch bag /'klʌtʃ bæg/ **53**
coach /kəʊtʃ/ **71**
coaster /'kəʊstəʳ/ **15**
coastline /'kəʊstlaɪn/ **117**
coat /kəʊt/ **46**
coat hanger /'kəʊt ˌhæŋəʳ/ **17**
cockatoo /kɒkəˈtuː/ **105**
cockerel /'kɒkərəl/ **102**
cockpit /'kɒkˌpɪt/ **77**
cockroach /'kɒkˌrəʊtʃ/ **106**
cocktail dress /'kɒkteɪl dres/ **47**
cocoa /'kəʊkəʊ/ **63**
coconut /'kəʊkənʌt/ **61**
cod fillet /kɒd ˈfɪlɪt/ **64**
coffee /'kɒfi/ **63, 66, 70**
coffee maker /'kɒfi ˌmeɪkəʳ/ **11**
coffee table /'.. ˌ../ **14**
coin /kɔɪn/ **94**
coin album /'kɔɪn ˌælbəm/ **94**
coin collecting /'kɔɪn kəˌlektɪŋ/ **94**
cola /'kəʊlə/ **63, 67**
cold /kəʊld/ **41, 118**
cold remedy /'kəʊld ˌremɪdi/ **42**
cold water tap /. '.. ./ **12**
coleslaw /'kəʊlslɔː/ **64**
collar /'kɒləʳ/ **50**
collection /kəˈlekʃən/ **82**
cologne /kəˈləʊn/ **40**
Colorado /ˌkɒləˈrɑːdəʊ/ **113**
coloured pen /ˌkʌləd ˈpen/ **83**
colouring book /'kʌlərɪŋ bʊk/ **55, 83**
colours /'kʌləz/ **51**
comb /kəʊm/ **39, 40**
comb your hair /ˌ. . ˈ./ **8**
comet /'kɒmɪt/ **119**
compact disc / CD player /ˌkɒmpækt ˈdɪsk ˌpleɪəʳ, siː ˈdiː ˌpleɪəʳ/ **122**
compass /'kʌmpəs/ **56**
compost /'kɒmpɒst‖ˈkɑːmpəʊst/ **19**
computer /kəmˈpjuːtəʳ/ **27, 56**
computer games /.ˈ.. ˌ./ **95, 120**
computer programmer /kəmˈpjuːtə ˈprəʊgræməʳ/ **26**

computer technician /kəmˌpjuːtə tekˈnɪʃən/ **26**
concierge /'kɒnsieəʒ/ **32**
condiments /'kɒndɪmənts/ **63**
conditioner /kənˈdɪʃənəʳ/ **12, 40**
conductor /kənˈdʌktəʳ/ **93**
cone /kəʊn/ **67**
confectionery /kənˈfekʃənəri/ **83**
conference room /'kɒnfərəns ruːm/ **32**
confused /kənˈfjuːzd/ **124**
conkers /'kɒŋkəz/ **117**
Connecticut /kəˈnetɪkət/ **113**
console /'kɒnsəʊl/ **120**
constellation /ˌkɒnstəˈleɪʃən/ **119**
construction worker /kənˈstrʌkʃən ˌwɜːkəʳ/ **31**
consultant /kənˈsʌltənt/ **44**
contact lens /'kɒntækt lenz/ **45**
container /kənˈteɪnəʳ/ **68**
continents /'kɒntɪnənts/ **114**
control pad /kənˈtrəʊl pæd/ **122**
control tower /kənˈtrəʊl ˌtaʊəʳ/ **77**
convertible /kənˈvɜːtəbəl/ **72**
conveyor belt /kənˈveɪə belt/ **30, 62**
cook /kʊk/ **21, 23, 69**
cookery /'kʊkəri/ **94**
cookery book /'... ./ **10**
cooking pot /'kʊkɪŋ pɒt/ **10**
cool /kuːl/ **118**
co-pilot /'kəʊ ˌpaɪlət/ **77**
cordless phone /ˌkɔːdləs ˈfəʊn/ **123**
coriander /ˌkɒriˈændəʳ/ **60**
Cork /kɔːk/ **112**
corn on the cob /ˌkɔːn ɒn ðə ˈkɒb/ **59**
corned beef /ˌkɔːnd ˈbiːf/ **62**
corner /'kɔːnəʳ/ **108**
correction fluid /kəˈrekʃən ˌfluːɪd/ **27, 83**
cosmetics /kɒzˈmetɪks/ **40**
cot /kɒt/ **16**
cottage /'kɒtɪdʒ/ **9**
cotton /'kɒtn/ **52**
couch /kaʊtʃ/ **39**
cough /kɒf/ **41**
cough mixture /'kɒf ˌmɪkstʃəʳ/ **42**
counsellor /'kaʊnsələʳ/ **43**
counter /'kaʊntəʳ/ **79, 82**
country code /'kʌntri kəʊd/ **85**
country of birth /ˌkʌntri əv ˈbɜːθ/ **6**
couple /'kʌpəl/ **6**
courgette /kʊəˈʒet/ **59**
court /kɔːt/ **88**
court reporter /ˌkɔːt rɪˈpɔːtəʳ/ **33**
courtroom /'kɔːtrʊm/ **33**
couscous /'kʊskʊs/ **63, 70**
cousins /'kʌzənz/ **7**

covering letter /ˌkʌvərɪŋ ˈletəʳ/ **22**
cow /kaʊ/ **102**
crab /kræb/ **64, 104**
craft fair /'krɑːft feəʳ/ **99**
crafts /krɑːfts/ **94**
cranberries /'krænbəriz/ **61**
crane /kreɪn/ **31, 78, 105**
crayons /'kreɪɒnz/ **55**
cream /kriːm/ **42, 51, 62, 66**
credit card /'kredɪt kɑːd/ **79**
crest /krest/ **105**
crewneck jumper /ˌkruːnek ˈdʒʌmpəʳ/ **46**
cricket /'krɪkɪt/ **86**
cricket ball /'.. ./ **86**
cricket pitch /'.. ./ **86**
crisps /krɪsps/ **67**
crockery /'krɒkəri/ **15**
crocodile /'krɒkədaɪl/ **103**
croissant /'kwaːsɒŋ/ **70**
cropped hair /ˌkrɒpt ˈheəʳ/ **36**
cross-country skiing /ˌkrɒs kʌntri ˈskiːɪŋ/ **91**
crossroads /'krɒsrəʊdz/ **74**
crossword /'krɒswɜːd/ **95**
crow /krəʊ/ **105**
crowd /kraʊd/ **86**
cruise ship /'kruːz ʃɪp/ **78**
crush /krʌʃ/ **69**
crutch /krʌtʃ/ **44**
cry /kraɪ/ **37**
cube /kjuːb/ **108**
cucumber /'kjuːkʌmbəʳ/ **59**
cuff /kʌf/ **50**
cuff link /'kʌf lɪŋk/ **53**
cup /kʌp/ **15**
cupboard /'kʌbəd/ **10**
cupful /'kʌpfʊl/ **68**
curly hair /ˌkɜːli ˈheəʳ/ **36**
cursor /'kɜːsəʳ/ **120**
curtain /'kɜːtn/ **14**
cushion /'kʊʃən/ **14**
customer /'kʌstəməʳ/ **62, 79**
customs /'kʌstəmz/ **76**
customs officer /'kʌstəmz ˌɒfɪsəʳ/ **76**
cut /kʌt/ **38, 39, 41**
cut up /ˌkʌt ˈʌp/ **69**
cutlery /'kʌtləri/ **15**
CV /ˌsiː ˈviː/ **22**
cycling /'saɪklɪŋ/ **89**
cycling shorts /'saɪklɪŋ ʃɔːts/ **49**
cyclist /'saɪklɪst/ **89**
cyclists only sign /'saɪklɪsts ˌəʊnli saɪn/ **75**
cylinder /'sɪlɪndəʳ/ **108**
cylinder block /'sɪlɪndə blɒk/ **72**
cymbal /'sɪmbəl/ **96**
Cyprus /'saɪprəs/ **116**
Czech Republic /ˌtʃek rɪˈpʌbklɪk/ **116**
daffodil /'dæfədɪl/ **18**
dairy products /'deəri ˌprɒdʌkts/ **62**
daisy /'deɪzi/ **18**
Dallas /'dæləs/ **113**
dam /dæm/ **117**
dance /dɑːns/ **37**
dark /dɑːk/ **125**

dark hair /ˌ. ˈ./ **36**
dashboard /ˈdæʃbɔːd/ **73**
date /deɪt/ **61**
date of birth /ˌdeɪt əv ˈbɜːθ/ **6**
daughter /ˈdɔːtər/ **7**
daughter-in-law /ˈdɔːtər ɪn lɔː/ **7**
days of the week /ˌdeɪz əv ðə ˈwiːk/ **109**
daytime telephone number / ˌdeɪtaɪm ˈtelɪfəʊn ˌnʌmbə/ **6**
debit card /ˈdebɪt kɑːd/ **79**
decay /dɪˈkeɪ/ **45**
December /dɪˈsembər/ **109**
deck /dek/ **78**
deckchair /ˈdektʃeər/ **97**
deep /diːp/ **125**
deer /dɪər/ **103**
defendant /dɪˈfendənt/ **33**
defenders /dɪˈfendəz/ **31**
degrees Celsius / degrees Centigrade /dɪˌgriːz ˈselsiəs, dɪˌgriːz ˈsentɪgreɪd/ **118**
degrees Fahrenheit /dɪˌgriːz ˈfærənhaɪt/ **118**
Delaware /ˈdeləweər/ **113**
delicatessen /ˌdelɪkəˈtesən/ **64**
delivery /dɪˈlɪvəri/ **82**
denim /ˈdenɪm/ **52**
Denmark /ˈdenmɑːk/ **116**
dental floss /ˈdentl flɒs/ **45**
dental nurse /ˈdentl nɜːs/ **45**
dentist /ˈdentɪst/ **24, 45**
dentures /ˈdentʃəz/ **45**
department store /dɪˈpɑːtmənt ˌstɔːr/ **80, 84**
departure gates /dɪˈpɑːtʃə ˌgeɪts/ **76**
deposit box / slot /dɪˈpɒzɪt bɒks, dɪˈpɒzɪt slɒt/ **79**
depth /depθ/ **108**
dermatologist / ˌdɜːməˈtɒlədʒɪst/ **43**
desert /ˈdezət/ **117**
design and technology /dɪˌzaɪn ən tekˈnɒlədʒi/ **57**
designer /dɪˈzaɪnər/ **25**
desk /desk/ **14, 27, 56**
desk diary /ˈdesk ˌdaɪəri/ **27**
desk lamp /ˈdesk læmp/ **27**
desk tidy /ˈdesk ˌtaɪdi/ **27**
dessert trolley /dɪˈzɜːt ˌtrɒli/ **65**
desserts /dɪˈzɜːts/ **66**
dessertspoon /dɪˈzɜːtspuːn/ **15**
detached house /dɪˈtætʃt ˈhaʊs/ **9**
diagonal /daɪˈægənəl/ **108**
dialling code /ˈdaɪəlɪŋ kəʊd/ **85**
diameter /daɪˈæmɪtər/ **108**
diamond /ˈdaɪəmənd/ **53**
dice /daɪs/ **95**
dictionary /ˈdɪkʃənəri/ **58**
dietician /ˌdaɪəˈtɪʃən/ **43**
dig the soil /ˌdɪg ðə ˈsɔɪl/ **19**
digger /ˈdɪgər/ **31**
digi-box /ˈdɪdʒi bɒks/ **122**
digital camera /ˌdɪdʒɪtl ˈkæmərə/ **123**
digital radio /ˌdɪdʒɪtl ˈreɪdiəʊ/ **122**

digital SLR camera /ˌdɪdʒɪtl es el ˈɑː ˌkæmərə/ **123**
digital watch /ˌdɪdʒɪtl ˈwɒtʃ/ **111**
dill /dɪl/ **60**
dim sum /dɪm ˈsʌm/ **65**
dining room /ˈdaɪnɪŋ ruːm/ **20**
dining room table /ˌ.. . ˈ../ **15**
dinner /ˈdɪnər/ **70**
dinner jacket /ˈ.. ˌ../ **48**
dishcloth /ˈdɪʃklɒθ/ **10**
dishwasher /ˈdɪʃˌwɒʃər/ **10**
display screen /dɪˈspleɪ skriːn/ **120**
distributor /dɪˈstrɪbjʊtər/ **72**
diver /ˈdaɪvər/ **90**
divided by /dɪˈvaɪdɪd baɪ/ **107**
diving /ˈdaɪvɪŋ/ **90**
diving board /ˈ.. ./ **90**
divorced /dɪˈvɔːst/ **6**
Diwali /dɪˈwɑːli/ **109**
DIY /ˌdiː aɪ ˈwaɪ/ **94**
do a handstand /duː ə ˈhændstænd/ **92**
do homework /duː ˈhəʊmwɜːk/ **21**
do press-ups /duː ˈpres ʌps/ **92**
do sit-ups /duː ˈsɪt ʌps/ **92**
do the laundry /duː ðə ˈlɔːndri/ **21**
dock /dɒk/ **78**
doctor /ˈdɒktər/ **24, 43**
doctor's surgery /ˌdɒktəz ˈsɜːdʒəri/ **43**
document /ˈdɒkjʊmənt/ **120**
document case /ˈdɒkjʊmənt ˌkeɪs/ **53**
dog /dɒg/ **101**
dog food /ˈdɒg fuːd/ **63**
doll /dɒl/ **55**
doll's pram /ˈdɒlz præm/ **55**
dolphin /ˈdɒlfɪn/ **104**
doner kebab /ˈdɒnə kɪˌbæb/ **67**
dongle /ˈdɒŋgəl/ **120**
donkey /ˈdɒŋki/ **102**
door /dɔːr/ **73**
door handle /ˈ. ../ **10**
doorbell /ˈdɔːbel/ **9**
doorknob /ˈdɔːnɒb/ **9**
doorstep /ˈdɔːstep/ **9**
dormitory /ˈdɔːmɪtəri/ **54**
double bass /ˌdʌbəl ˈbeɪs/ **96**
double bed /ˌdʌbəl ˈbed/ **13**
double oven /ˌdʌbəl ˈʌvən/ **10**
double room /ˌdʌbəl ruːm/ **32**
double yellow line /ˌdʌbəl jeləʊ ˈlaɪn/ **80**
doughnut /ˈdəʊnʌt/ **67**
Dover /ˈdəʊvər/ **112**
down /daʊn/ **126**
downhill skiing /ˌdaʊnhɪl ˈskiːɪŋ/ **91**
Downing Street /ˈdaʊnɪŋ striːt/ **100**
downstairs /ˌdaʊnˈsteəz/ **20**
dragonfly /ˈdrægənflaɪ/ **106**
drainpipe /ˈdreɪnpaɪp/ **9**
drape AmE /dreɪp/ **14**
draughts /drɑːfts/ **95**
draughtsman /ˈdrɑːftsmən/ **25**
draw /drɔː/ **38**

drawer /drɔːr/ **10, 13**
drawing pins /ˈdrɔːɪŋ pɪnz/ **83**
dress /dres/ **47**
dressing gown /ˈdresɪŋ gaʊn/ **47**
dressing table /ˈdresɪŋ ˌteɪbəl/ **13**
dressmaker /ˈdresˌmeɪkər/ **52**
drill /drɪl/ **45**
drill bits /ˈdrɪl bɪts/ **29**
drinks /drɪŋks/ **63, 66**
drip /drɪp/ **85**
drive /draɪv/ **9**
driving licence /ˈdraɪvɪŋ ˌlaɪsəns/ **6**
drum /drʌm/ **96**
drum kit /ˈdrʌm kɪt/ **96**
dry /draɪ/ **125**
dry goods /ˈdraɪ gʊdz/ **63**
dry yourself /ˈdraɪ jəself/ **8**
dual carriageway /ˌdjuːəl ˈkærɪdʒweɪ/ **74**
Dublin /ˈdʌblɪn/ **112**
duck /dʌk/ **102**
duckling /ˈdʌklɪŋ/ **102**
dummy /ˈdʌmi/ **16**
dumper truck /ˈdʌmpə trʌk/ **31**
Dun Laoghaire /dʌn ˈlɪəri/ **112**
Dundee /dʌnˈdi/ **112**
dungarees /ˌdʌŋgəˈriːz/ **48**
Durham /ˈdʌrəm/ **112**
dust /dʌst/ **21**
duster /ˈdʌstər/ **17**
dustpan /ˈdʌstpæn/ **17**
duty-free shop /ˌdjuːti ˈfriː ʃɒp/ **76**
duvet /ˈduːveɪ, ˈdjuː-/ **13**
DVD /ˌdiː viː ˈdiː/ **122**
DVD player /ˌ. .ˈ. ../ **14, 56, 122**
eagle /ˈiːgəl/ **105**
ear /ɪər/ **34**
ear protectors /ˈɪə prəˌtektəz/ **31**
ear, nose, throat specialist /ɪə nəʊz ˈθrəʊt speʃəlɪst/ **43**
earring /ˈɪərɪŋ/ **53**
Earth /ɜːθ/ **119**
easel /ˈiːzəl/ **55**
Easter Sunday /ˌiːstə ˈsʌndeɪ/ **109**
ecstatic /ɪkˈstætɪk/ **124**
edge /edʒ/ **108**
Edinburgh /ˈedɪnbərə/ **112**
Edinburgh Castle /ˌedɪnbərə ˈkɑːsəl/ **100**
eel /iːl/ **104**
egg /eg/ **105**
eggs /egz/ **62**
Eid ul-Fitr /ˌiːd ʊl ˈfɪtrə/ **109**
eight /eɪt/ **107**
eight am / eight (o'clock) in the morning /ˌeɪt eɪ ˈem, ˌeɪt əklɒk ɪn ðə ˈmɔːnɪŋ/ **111**
eight pm / eight (o'clock) in the evening /ˌeɪt piː ˈem, ˌeɪt əklɒk ɪn ði ˈiːvnɪŋ/ **111**
eighteen /ˌeɪˈtiːn/ **107**
eighteen hundred hours /ˌeɪtiːn ˈhʌndrəd aʊəz/ **111**
eighty /ˈeɪti/ **107**

elastic band /ɪˌlæstɪk ˈbænd/ **27**
elbow /ˈelbəʊ/ **34**
elderly /ˈeldəli/ **6**
electric drill /ɪˌlektrɪk ˈdrɪl/ **29**
electric guitar /ɪˌlektrɪk gɪˈtɑːr/ **96**
electric mixer /ɪˌlektrɪk ˈmɪksər/ **11**
electric shaver /ɪˌlektrɪk ˈʃeɪvər/ **40**
electric typewriter /ɪˌlektrɪk ˈtaɪpˌraɪtər/ **27**
electric window button / ɪˌlektrɪk ˈwɪndəʊ ˌbʌtn/ **73**
electrician /ɪˌlekˈtrɪʃən, ˌelɪk-/ **23**
electronic games /ˌelɪktrɒnɪk ˈgeɪmz/ **120**
electronic personal organiser / ˌelɪktrɒnɪk ˌpɜːsənəl ˈɔːgənaɪzər/ **123**
electronics shop /ɪˌlekˈtrɒnɪks ʃɒp/ **84**
elephant /ˈelɪfənt/ **103**
elevator AmE /ˈeləveɪtər/ **32**
eleven /ɪˈlevən/ **107**
eleven hundred hours /ɪˌlevən ˈhʌndrəd aʊəz/ **111**
e-mail /ˈiː meɪl/ **121**
e-mail address /ˈiː meɪl əˌdres‖ˌædres/ **6, 22, 121**
e-mail software /ˈiː meɪl ˈsɒftweər/ **121**
embroidery /ɪmˈbrɔɪdəri/ **94**
emerald /ˈemərəld/ **53**
emergency number / ɪˈmɜːdʒənsi ˌnʌmbər/ **85**
emery board /ˈeməri bɔːd/ **40**
empty /ˈempti/ **68, 125**
en suite shower room /ɒn swiːt ˈʃaʊə ruːm/ **20**
encyclopedia /ɪnˌsaɪkləˈpiːdiə/ **58**
engine /ˈendʒɪn/ **71, 72**
England /ˈɪŋglənd/ **112**
english /ˈɪŋglɪʃ/ **57**
English breakfast /ˌɪŋglɪʃ ˈbrekfəst/ **70**
envelope /ˈenvələʊp/ **82**
equals /ˈiːkwəlz/ **107**
e-reader /ˈiː ˌriːdər/ **122**
escalator /ˈeskəleɪtər/ **84**
estate agent /ɪˈsteɪt ˌeɪdʒənt/ **25**
estate car /ɪˈsteɪt kɑːr/ **72**
Estonia /eˈstəʊniə/ **116**
European Union /ˌjʊərpiən ˈjuːnjən/ **116**
euros /ˈjʊərəʊz/ **79**
evening gown /ˈiːvnɪŋ gaʊn/ **47**
evidence /ˈevɪdəns/ **33**
examination couch / ɪgˌzæmɪˈneɪʃən kaʊtʃ/ **43**
excavation site /ˌekskəˈveɪʃən saɪt/ **31**
excavator /ˈekskəveɪtər/ **31**
exchange rates /ɪksˈtʃeɪndʒ reɪts/ **79**

exercise bike /ˈeksəsaɪz baɪk/ **92**

exercise book /ˈeksəsaɪz bʊk/ **56**

exhaust pipe /ɪgˈzɔːst paɪp/ **73**

exhibition /ˌeksɪˈbɪʃən/ **99**

ex-husband /eks ˈhʌzbənd/ **7**

expensive /ɪkˈspensɪv/ **125**

external hard drive /ɪkˈstɜːnl ˈhɑːd draɪv/ **120**

ex-wife /ˌeks ˈwaɪf/ **7**

eye /aɪ/ **34**

eye drops /ˈaɪ drɒps/ **42, 45**

eye shadow /ˈaɪ ˌʃædəʊ/ **40**

eyebrow /ˈaɪbraʊ/ **35**

eyebrow pencil /ˈ.. ˌ../ **40**

eyelash /ˈaɪlæʃ/ **35**

eyelid /ˈaɪlɪd/ **35**

eyeliner /ˈaɪ ˌlaɪnəʳ/ **40**

fabric conditioner /ˈfæbrɪk kənˌdɪʃənəʳ/ **17**

fabric shop /ˈfæbrɪk ʃɒp/ **84**

face /feɪs/ **34, 108, 111**

facecloth /ˈfeɪsklɒθ/ **12**

facial /ˈfeɪʃəl/ **39**

factory worker /ˈfæktəri ˌwɜːkəʳ/ **25**

fair hair /ˌfeəʳ ˈheəʳ/ **36**

fajitas /fəˈhiːtəz/ **65**

falafel /fəˈlæfəl/ **67**

falcon /ˈfɔːlkən/ **105**

fall /fɔːl/ **37, 92**

fall AmE /fɔːl/ **118**

family name /ˈfæməli neɪm/ **6**

fans /fænz/ **86**

far /fɑːʳ/ **125**

farmer /ˈfɑːməʳ/ **23**

fashion store /ˈfæʃən stɔːʳ/ **84**

fast /fɑːst/ **125**

father /ˈfɑːðəʳ/ **7**

Father's Day /ˈfɑːðəz deɪ/ **109**

father-in-law /ˈfɑːðər ɪn lɔː/ **7**

fatty tissue /ˌfæti ˈtɪʃuː/ **35**

faucet AmE /ˈfɔːsɪt/ **10**

fax a document /ˌfæks ə ˈdɒkjumənt/ **28**

fax machine /ˈfæks məˌʃiːn/ **27**

feathers /ˈfeðəz/ **105**

February /ˈfebruəri/ **109**

feed the baby /ˌ.. ˈ../ **21**

feed the dog /ˌfiːd ðə ˈdɒg/ **21**

feelings /ˈfiːlɪŋz/ **124**

fence /fens/ **9, 19**

fennel /ˈfenl/ **60**

ferry /ˈferi/ **78**

fertiliser /ˈfɜːtɪlaɪzəʳ/ **19**

festivals /ˈfestɪvəlz/ **109**

field /fiːld/ **117**

fielder /ˈfiːldəʳ/ **86**

fifteen /fɪfˈtiːn/ **107**

fifteen hundred hours /ˌfɪftiːn ˈhʌndrəd ˌaʊəz/ **111**

fifth /fɪfθ/ **107**

fifty /ˈfɪfti/ **107**

fifty pence / fifty pence piece /ˌfɪfti ˈpens, ˌfɪfti pens ˈpiːs/ **79**

fifty percent /ˌfɪfti pəˈsent/ **107**

fifty pounds / fifty pound note /ˌfɪfti ˈpaʊndz, ˌfɪfti paʊnd ˈnəʊt/ **79**

fig /fɪg/ **61**

figure skate /ˈfɪgə skeɪt/ **91**

figure skater /ˈfɪgə ˌskeɪtəʳ/ **91**

figure skating /ˈfɪgə ˌskeɪtɪŋ/ **91**

file /faɪl/ **29, 120**

file attachment /ˈfaɪl əˌtætʃmənt/ **121**

file papers /ˌfaɪl ˈpeɪpəz/ **28**

files /faɪlz/ **27**

filing cabinet /ˈfaɪlɪŋ ˌkæbɪnət/ **28**

fill /fɪl/ **38**

fill in a form /ˌfɪl ɪn ə ˈfɔːm/ **28**

fillet of sole /ˌfɪlɪt əv ˈsəʊl/ **65**

filling /ˈfɪlɪŋ/ **45**

film /fɪlm/ **93, 123**

Filofax™ /ˈfaɪləʊ ˌfæks/ **53**

fin /fɪn/ **104**

financial adviser /fəˌnænʃəl ədˈvaɪzə/ **79**

finger /ˈfɪŋgə/ **34**

Finland /ˈfɪnlənd/ **116**

fir cone /ˈfɜː kəʊn/ **117**

fir tree /ˈfɜː triː/ **117**

fire /faɪəʳ/ **85**

fire brigade /ˈfaɪə brɪˌgeɪd/ **85**

fire engine /ˈ. ˌ../ **85**

fire extinguisher /ˈfaɪər ɪkˌstɪŋgwɪʃəʳ/ **30, 85**

fire fighter /ˈfaɪə ˌfaɪtəʳ/ **24, 85**

fireguard /ˈfaɪəgɑːd/ **14**

fireplace /ˈfaɪəpleɪs/ **14**

first /fɜːst/ **107**

first class /ˌfɜːst ˈklɑːs/ **71**

first class post /ˌfɜːst klɑːs ˈpəʊst/ **82**

first floor /ˌ. ˈ./ **20**

first name /ˈ. ./ **6**

first-aid kit /ˌfɜːst ˈeɪd kɪt/ **30**

fish /fɪʃ/ **104**

fish and chips /ˌfɪʃ ən ˈtʃɪps/ **67**

fish and seafood /ˌfɪʃ ən ˈsiːfuːd/ **64**

fish fingers /ˌfɪʃ ˈfɪŋgəz/ **62, 70**

fish tank /ˈfɪʃ tæŋk/ **101**

fisherman /ˈfɪʃəmən/ **23, 90**

fishing /ˈfɪʃɪŋ/ **90**

fishing hook /ˈ.. ˌ../ **98**

fishing line /ˈfɪʃɪŋ laɪn/ **90**

fishing rod /ˈfɪʃɪŋ rɒd/ **90, 98**

fitted sheet /ˌfɪtɪd ˈʃiːt/ **13**

five /faɪv/ **107**

five pence / five pence piece /ˌfaɪv ˈpens, ˌfaɪv pens ˈpiːs/ **79**

five pounds / five pound note /ˌfaɪv ˈpaʊndz, ˌtuː paʊnd ˈnəʊt/ **79**

fizzy drink /ˌfɪzi drɪŋk/ **67**

fizzy mineral water /ˌfɪzi ˈmɪnərəl ˌwɔːtəʳ/ **66**

flag /flæg/ **81, 119**

flamingo /fləˈmɪŋgəʊ/ **105**

flannel /ˈflænl/ **12**

flash /flæʃ/ **123**

flats /flæts/ **9**

flatscreen TV /ˌflætskriːn tiː ˈviː/ **122**

fleece /fliːs/ **46**

flight attendant /ˌflaɪt əˈtendənt/ **77**

flight information screens /ˌflaɪt ɪnfəˈmeɪʃən ˌskriːnz/ **76**

flip-flops /ˈflɪp flɒps/ **47**

flipper /ˈflɪpəʳ/ **104, 105**

floor /flɔːʳ/ **20**

Florida /ˈflɒrɪdə/ **113**

florist /ˈflɒrɪst/ **23**

flour /flaʊəʳ/ **63**

flowerbed /ˈflaʊəbed/ **18**

flowers /ˈflaʊəz/ **14, 18**

flu /fluː/ **41**

flute /fluːt/ **96**

fly /flaɪ/ **106**

flyover /ˈflaɪ-əʊvəʳ/ **74**

foal /fəʊl/ **102**

foggy /ˈfɒgi/ **118**

fold /fəʊld/ **38**

folder /ˈfəʊldəʳ/ **27, 120**

font /fɒnt/ **120**

food processor /ˈfuːd ˌprəʊsesəʳ/ **11**

foot /fʊt/ **34**

football /ˈfʊtbɔːl/ **86**

football boots /ˈ.. ˌ../ **86**

footballer /ˈfʊtbɔːləʳ/ **86**

footrest /ˈfʊt-rest/ **39**

footwear /ˈfʊtweəʳ/ **47**

forearm /ˈfɔːrɑːm/ **34**

forehead /ˈfɒrɪd, ˈfɔːhed/ **35**

foreign currency /ˌfɒrɪn ˈkʌrənsi/ **79**

foreman /ˈfɔːmən/ **30**

forest /ˈfɒrɪst/ **117**

fork /fɔːk/ **15, 19**

forklift /ˈfɔːklɪft/ **30**

formal wear /ˈfɔːməl weəʳ/ **47, 48**

forty /ˈfɔːti/ **107**

foundation /faʊnˈdeɪʃən/ **40**

fountain pen /ˈfaʊntɪn pen/ **83**

four /fɔːʳ/ **107**

fourteen /fɔːˈtiːn/ **107**

fourth /fɔːθ/ **107**

four-wheel drive /ˌfɔː wiːl ˈdraɪv/ **72**

fox /fɒks/ **103**

foyer /ˈfɔɪeɪ/ **32**

frame /freɪm/ **45**

France /frɑːns/ **116**

franking machine /ˈfræŋkɪŋ məˌʃiːn/ **27**

freezer /ˈfriːzəʳ/ **10**

freezing /ˈfriːzɪŋ/ **118**

freight lift /ˈfreɪt lɪft/ **30**

French /frentʃ/ **57**

French bean /ˌfrentʃ ˈbiːn/ **59**

French fries /ˌfrentʃ ˈfraɪz/ **67**

French horn /ˌfrentʃ ˈhɔːn/ **96**

Friday /ˈfraɪddi/ **109**

fridge /frɪdʒ/ **10**

fried chicken /ˌfraɪd ˈtʃɪkɪn/ **67**

fringe /frɪndʒ/ **36**

frog /frɒg/ **103**

from /frɒm/ **126**

front door /ˌfrʌnt ˈdɔːʳ/ **9**

front garden /ˌfrʌnt ˈgɑːdn/ **9**

front teeth /ˌfrʌnt ˈtiːθ/ **45**

frown /fraʊn/ **37**

frozen foods /ˌfrəʊzən ˈfuːdz/ **62**

fry /fraɪ/ **69**

frying pan /ˈfraɪ-ɪŋ pæn/ **11**

fudge /fʌdʒ/ **83**

fuel gauge /ˈfjuːəl geɪdʒ/ **73**

fuel tank /ˈfjuːəl tæŋk/ **119**

full /fʊl/ **68, 125**

full cream milk /ˌfʊl kriːm ˈmɪlk/ **70**

full moon /ˌfʊl ˈmuːn/ **119**

fur /fɜːʳ/ **101**

furious /ˈfjʊəriəs/ **124**

galaxy /ˈgæləksi/ **119**

Galway /ˈgɔːlweɪ/ **112**

gamepad /ˈgeɪmpæd/ **120**

games /geɪmz/ **95**

games console /. ˌ../ **122**

garage /ˈgærɑːʒ/gəˈrɑːʒ/ **9, 72**

garden shed /ˌgɑːdn ˈʃed/ **18**

gardener /ˈgɑːdnəʳ/ **23**

gardening /ˈgɑːdnɪŋ/ **94**

gardening gloves /ˈgɑːdnɪŋ ˌglʌvz/ **19**

garlic /ˈgɑːlɪk/ **59**

garlic press /ˈ.. ˌ../ **11**

gate /geɪt/ **9, 87**

gauze pad /ˈgɔːz pæd/ **42**

gear lever/stick /ˈgɪə ˌliːvəʳ, ˈgɪə stɪk/ **73**

gear shift AmE /ˈgɪə ʃɪft/ **73**

gems /dʒemz/ **53**

general practitioner (GP) /ˌdʒenərəl prækˈtɪʃənəʳ, ˌdʒiː ˈpiː/ **43**

geography /dʒiˈɒgrəfi/ **57**

Georgia /ˈdʒɔːdʒə/ **113**

geranium /dʒəˈreɪniəm/ **18**

gerbil /ˈdʒɜːbəl/ **101**

German /ˈdʒɜːmən/ **57**

Germany /ˈdʒɜːməni/ **116**

get dressed /ˌget ˈdrest/ **8**

get up /ˌget ˈʌp/ **8**

gherkins /ˈgɜːkɪnz/ **67**

gills /gɪlz/ **104**

ginger hair /ˌdʒɪndʒə ˈheəʳ/ **36**

giraffe /dʒɪˈrɑːf/ **103**

girder /ˈgɜːdəʳ/ **31**

girl /gɜːl/ **6**

give /gɪv/ **38**

give way sign /ˈgɪv weɪ saɪn/ **75**

Glasgow /ˈglæzgəʊ/ **112**

glasses /ˈglɑːsɪz/ **45**

glasses case /ˈglɑːsɪz keɪs/ **45**

glove /glʌv/ **87**

gloves /glʌvz/ **46**

glue /gluː/ **38, 55**

go shopping /ˌgəʊ ˈʃɒpɪŋ/ **21**

go to bed /ˌgəʊ tə ˈbed/ **8**

go to work /ˌgəʊ tə ˈwɜːk/ **8**

goal /gəʊl/ **86**

goal area /ˈgəʊl ˌeəriə/ **86**

goal line /ˈgəʊl laɪn/ **86**

goalie /ˈgəʊli/ **86**

goalkeeper /ˈgəʊlˌkiːpəʳ/ **86**

goalpost /ˈgəʊlpəʊst/ **86**

goatee /gəʊˈtiː/ **36**

goggles /ˈgɒgəlz/ **90**

gold /gəʊld/ **53**

goldfish /ˈgəʊldˌfɪʃ/ **101**

metal detector /ˈmetl dɪˌtektəʳ/ 76

metals /ˈmetlz/ 53

metre /ˈmiːtəʳ/ 68

Miami /maɪˈæmi/ 113

Michigan /ˈmɪʃɪgən/ 113

microfiche /ˈmaɪkrəʊfiːʃ/ 58

microfiche reader /ˈmaɪkrəʊfiːʃ ˌriːdəʳ/ 58

microphone /ˈmaɪkrəfəʊn/ 96

microwave /ˈmaɪkrəweɪv/ 11

middle lane /ˌmɪdl ˈleɪn/ 74

midwife /ˈmɪdwaɪf/ 26

mike /maɪk/ 96

millilitres /ˈmɪlɪˌliːtəz/ 68

milk /mɪlk/ 62, 66

milk shake /ˈmɪlk ˌʃeɪk/ 67

millimetre /ˈmɪlɪmiːtəʳ/ 68

minced beef /ˌmɪnst ˈbiːf/ 64

mineral water /ˈmɪnərəl ˌwɔːtəʳ/ 63

minibus /ˈmɪnibʌs/ 72

minicab /ˈminikæb/ 71

Minnesota /ˌmɪnəˈsəʊtə/ 113

mint /mɪnt/ 60

mints /mɪnts/ 83

minus /ˈmaɪnəs/ 107

minute hand /ˈmɪnɪt hænd/ 111

mirror /ˈmɪrəʳ/ 12, 13, 39, 45

miserable /ˈmɪzərəbəl/ 124

missing button /ˌmɪsɪŋ ˈbʌtn/ 52

Mississippi /ˌmɪsɪˈsɪpi/ 113

Mississippi River /ˌ.... ˈ../ 113

Missouri /mɪˈzʊəri/ 113

Missouri River /.ˌ.. ˈ../ 113

mix /mɪks/ 69

mixed vegetables /ˌmɪkst ˈvedʒtəbəlz/ 66

mixing bowl /ˈmɪksɪŋ bəʊl/ 11

mobile /ˈməʊbaɪl/ 16, 123

mobile phone number /ˈməʊbaɪl ˈfəʊn ˌnʌmbəʳ/ 6

mobile phone shop /ˌməʊbaɪl ˈfəʊn ʃɒp/ 84

moisturiser /ˈmɔɪstʃəraɪzəʳ/ 40

mole /məʊl/ 106

Monday /ˈmʌndei/ 109

money clip /ˈmʌni klɪp/ 53

monitor /ˈmɒnɪtəʳ/ 120

monk /mʌŋk/ 110

monkey /ˈmʌŋki/ 103

Monopoly™ /məˈnɒpəli/ 95

Montana /mɒnˈtænə/ 113

months /mʌnθs/ 109

moon /muːn/ 119

mop /mɒp/ 17

mosque /mɒsk/ 110

mosquito /mɒˈskiːtəʊ/ 106

moth /mɒθ/ 106

mother /ˈmʌðəʳ/ 7

Mother's Day /ˈmʌðəz dei/ 109

mother-in-law /ˈmʌðər ɪn lɔː/ 7

motor boat /ˈməʊtə bəʊt/ 78

motor scooter /ˈməʊtə ˌskuːtəʳ/ 72

motorbike /ˈməʊtəbaɪk/ 72

motorboat /ˈməʊtəbəʊt/ 90

motorcycle courier /ˈməʊtəˌsaɪkəl ˌkʊriəʳ/ 23

motorway /ˈməʊtəwei/ 74

mountain /ˈmaʊntɪn/ 117

mouse /maʊs/ 106, 120

mouse mat /ˈmaʊs mæt/ 120

moussaka /mʊˈsɑːkə/ 65

moustache /məˈstɑːʃ‖ˈmʌstæʃ/ 36

mouth /maʊθ/ 34

mouthwash /ˈmaʊθwɒʃ/ 45

movie AmE /ˈmuːvi/ 93

mow the lawn /ˌməʊ ðə ˈlɔːn/ 19

MP3 player /ˌem piː ˈθri ˌpleɪəʳ/ 122

muesli /ˈmjuːzli/ 70

muffin /ˈmʌfɪn/ 67

mug /mʌg/ 12, 15

muscles /ˈmʌsəlz/ 35

museum /mjuːˈziːəm/ 99

mushroom /ˈmʌʃrʊm/ 59

mushroom risotto /ˌmʌʃrʊm rɪˈzɒtəʊ/ 70

music /ˈmjuːzɪk/ 57

music and entertainment shop /ˌmjuːzɪk ənd ˌentəˈteɪnmənt ʃɒp/ 84

music stand /ˈmjuːzɪk stænd/ 93

Muslim /ˈmʊzlɪm/ 110

mussels /ˈmʌsəlz/ 64, 104

mustard /ˈmʌstəd/ 63, 67

naan bread /ˈnɑːn bred/ 64

nacho chips /ˈnætʃəʊ ˌtʃɪps/ 65

nail /neɪl/ 34

nail clippers /ˈneɪl ˌklɪpəz/ 40

nail file /ˈneɪl faɪl/ 40

nail polish /ˈneɪl ˌpɒlɪʃ/ 40

nail scissors /ˈneɪl ˌsɪzəz/ 40

nails /neɪlz/ 29

name /neɪm/ 6

nanny /ˈnæni/ 26

nanny goat /ˈnæni gəʊt/ 102

napkin /ˈnæpkɪn/ 15

napkin ring /ˈnæpkɪn rɪŋ/ 15

nappy /ˈnæpi/ 16

narrow /ˈnærəʊ/ 50, 125

National Insurance number /ˌnæʃənəl ɪnˈʃʊərəns ˌnʌmbəʳ/ 6

nationality /ˌnæʃəˈnæliti/ 6

nature reserve /ˈneɪtʃə rɪˌzɜːv/ 98

navy blue /ˌneɪvi ˈbluː/ 51

near /nɪəʳ/ 125

neat /niːt/ 125

Nebraska /nɪˈbræskə/ 113

neck /nek/ 34

neck and shoulder massage /ˌnek ən ˈʃəʊldə ˌmæsɑːʒ/ 39

necklace /ˈneklɪs/ 53

nectarine /ˈnektəriːn/ 61

needle /ˈniːdl/ 44, 52

nephew /ˈnefjuː/ 7

Neptune /ˈneptjuːn/ 119

nervous /ˈnɜːvəs/ 124

nest /nest/ 105

net /net/ 86, 87, 88

Netherlands /ˈneðələndz/ 116

network /ˈnetwɜːk/ 121

network engineer /ˈnetwɜːk ˌendʒɪˌnɪəʳ/ 26

Nevada /nəˈvɑːdə/ 113

New Hampshire /njuː ˈhæmpʃəʳ/ 113

New Jersey /njuː ˈdʒɜːzi/ 113

New Mexico /njuː ˈmeksɪkəʊ/ 113

new moon /njuː ˈmuːn/ 119

New Orleans /njuː ˈɔːliənz/ 113

New Year's Eve /ˌnjuː jɪəz ˈiːv/ 109

New York /njuː ˈjɔːk/ 113

Newcastle-upon-Tyne /ˌnjuːkɑːsəl əpɒn ˈtaɪn/ 112

newspaper /ˈnjuːsˌpeɪpəʳ/ 83

newspaper stand /ˈnjuːspeɪpə ˌstænd/ 81

newspaper vendor /ˈnjuːspeɪpə ˌvendəʳ/ 81

newsreader /ˈnjuːzˌriːdəʳ/ 25

next of kin /ˌnekst əv ˈkɪn/ 6

next to /ˈnekst tuː/ 127

niece /niːs/ 7

nightclothes /ˈnaɪtkləʊðz/ 47

nightdress /ˈnaɪtdres/ 47

nightie /ˈnaɪti/ 47

nil /nɪl/ 107

nine /naɪn/ 107

nineteen /ˌnaɪnˈtiːn/ 107

nineteen forty-five /ˌ... .. ˈ./ 111

nineteen thirty /ˌnaɪntiːn ˈθɜːti/ 111

ninety /ˈnaɪnti/ 107

no overtaking sign /nəʊ əʊvəˈteɪkɪŋ saɪn/ 75

no right turn sign /nəʊ raɪt ˈtɜːn saɪn/ 75

no through road sign /nəʊ θruː ˈrəʊd saɪn/ 75

no U-turn sign /nəʊ ˈjuː tɜːn saɪn/ 75

North America /ˌnɔːθ əˈmerɪkə/ 114

North Carolina /ˌnɔːθ kærəˈlaɪnə/ 113

North Dakota /ˌnɔːθ dəˈkəʊtə/ 113

Northern Ireland /ˌnɔːðən ˈaɪələnd/ 112

nose /nəʊz/ 34

nose bleed /ˈnəʊz bliːd/ 41

note appointments /ˌnəʊt əˈpɔɪntmənts/ 28

notepad /ˈnəʊtpæd/ 27

noticeboard /ˈnəʊtɪsˌbɔːd/ 27

Nottingham /ˈnɒtɪŋəm/ 112

nought /nɔːt/ 107

November /nəʊˈvembəʳ/ 109

nozzle /ˈnɒzəl/ 72

number pad /ˈnʌmbə pæd/ 85

numberplate /ˈnʌmbəpleɪt/ 73

nurse /nɜːs/ 24, 43, 44

nursery assistant /ˈnɜːsəri əˌsɪstənt/ 24

nursery school /ˈnɜːsəri skuːl/ 54

nut /nʌt/ 29

nuts and raisins /ˌnʌts ənd ˈreɪzənz/ 67

oak tree /ˈəʊk triː/ 117

oar /ɔːʳ/ 78, 90

oarsman /ˈɔːzmən/ 90

oarswoman /ˈɔːzˌwʊmən/ 90

oats /əʊts/ 63

oboe /ˈəʊbəʊ/ 96

obstetrician /ˌɒbstəˈtrɪʃən/ 43

obtuse angle /əbˈtjuːs ˌæŋgəl/ 108

ocean AmE /ˈəʊʃən/ 97

October /ɒkˈtəʊbəʳ/ 109

octopus /ˈɒktəpəs/ 104

off /ɒf/ 126

offer refreshments /ˌɒfə rɪˈfreʃmənts/ 28

office worker /ˈɒfɪs ˌwɜːkəʳ/ 25

offices /ˈɒfɪsɪz/ 80

Ohio /əʊˈhaɪəʊ/ 113

oil /ɔɪl/ 63

oil tanker /ˈɔɪl ˌtæŋkəʳ/ 78

Oklahoma /ˌəʊkləˈhəʊmə/ 113

okra /ˈɒkrə/ 60

old /əʊld/ 6

olives /ˈɒlɪvz/ 67

omelette /ˈɒmlət/ 70

on /ɒn/ 126

on board /ɒn ˈbɔːd/ 77

on top of /. ˈ. ../ 127

one /wʌn/ 107

one half /wʌn ˈhɑːf/ 68

one hundred /wʌn ˈhʌndrəd/ 107

one hundred and one /wʌn ˈhʌndrəd ən ˈwʌn/ 107

one hundred percent /wʌn ˌhʌndrəd pəˈsent/ 107

one hundred thousand /wʌn ˈhʌndrəd ˈθaʊzənd/ 107

one million /wʌn ˈmɪljən/ 107

one penny / one penny piece /ˌwʌn ˈpeni, ˌwʌn peni ˈpiːs/ 79

one pound / one pound coin /ˌwʌn ˈpaʊnd, ˌwʌn paʊnd ˈkɔɪn/ 79

one quarter /wʌn ˈkwɔːtəʳ/ 68

one third /wʌn ˈθɜːd/ 68

one thousand /wʌn ˈθaʊzənd/ 107

onion /ˈʌnjən/ 59

online banking /ˌɒnlaɪn ˈbæŋkɪŋ/ 79

onto /ˈɒntuː/ 126

open /ˈəʊpən/ 38, 125

opera /ˈɒprə/ 93

operating theatre /ˈɒpəreɪtɪŋ ˌθɪətəʳ/ 44

operation /ˌɒpəˈreɪʃən/ 44

ophthalmologist /ˌɒfθælˈmɒlədʒɪst/ 43

opposites /ˈɒpəzɪts/ 125

optician /ɒpˈtɪʃən/ 24, 45

optician's /ɒpˈtɪʃənz/ 84

oral hygienist /ˌɔːrəl ˈhaɪdʒiːnɪst/ 45

orange /ˈɒrɪndʒ/ 51, 61

orange juice /ˈɒrɪndʒ dʒuːs/ 63, 67

orbit /ˈɔːbɪt/ 119

orchestra pit /ˈɔːkɪstrə pɪt/ 93

orchid /ˈɔːkɪd/ 18

oregano /ˌɒrɪˈgɑːnəʊ/ 60

Oregon /ˈɒrɪgən/ 113

WORD LIST

scientist /ˈsaɪəntɪst/ 24
scissors /ˈsɪzəz/ 39, 52, 82
scooter /ˈskuːtəʳ/ 55
scoreboard /ˈskɔːbɔːd/ 86
Scotland /ˈskɒtlənd/ 112
Scottish Parliament /ˌskɒtɪʃ ˈpɑːləmənt/ 100
Scrabble™ /ˈskræbəl/ 95
scratch /skrætʃ/ 41
screwdriver /ˈskruːdraɪvəʳ/ 29
screws /skruːz/ 29
scrubbing brush /ˈskrʌbɪŋ brʌʃ/ 17
scuba diver /ˈskuːbə ˌdaɪvəʳ/ 90
scuba diving /ˈskuːbə ˌdaɪvɪŋ/ 90
sculpting /ˈskʌlptɪŋ/ 94
sculpture /ˈskʌlptʃəʳ/ 94
sea /siː/ 97
sea animals /ˈsiː ˌænɪməlz/ 104
seal /siːl/ 104
seam /siːm/ 50
search engine /ˈsɜːtʃ ˌendʒɪn/ 121
search page /ˈsɜːtʃ peɪdʒ/ 121
seasons /ˈsiːzənz/ 118
seat belt /ˈsiːt belt/ 73
Seattle /siˈætl/ 113
secateurs /ˈsekətɜːz/ 19
second /ˈsekənd/ 107
second class /ˌsekənd ˈklɑːs/ 71
second class post /ˌsekənd klɑːs ˈpəʊst/ 82
second floor /ˌsekənd ˈflɔːʳ/ 20
second hand /ˈsekənd hænd/ 111
secondary school /ˈsekəndəri ˌskuːl/ 54, 57
secretary /ˈsekrɪtəri/ 25
security /sɪˈkjʊərəti/ 76
security guard /sɪˈkjʊərəti ˌgɑːd/ 26
seed trays /ˈsiːd treɪz/ 19
seeds /siːdz/ 19
seesaw /ˈsiːsɔː/ 55
self-checkout area /self ˈʃekaʊt ˌeəriə/ 62
Sellotape™ /ˈseləteɪp/ 27, 83
semi-detached house /ˌsemi dɪˈtætʃt ˈhaʊs/ 9
semi-skimmed milk /ˌsemi skɪmd ˈmɪlk/ 70
send a fax /ˌsend ə ˈfæks/ 28
send an e-mail /ˌsend ən ˈiːmeɪl/ 28
September /sepˈtembəʳ/ 109
sequins /ˈsiːkwɪnz/ 52
server /ˈsɜːvəʳ/ 121
serviette /ˌsɜːviˈet/ 15
serving dish /ˈsɜːvɪŋ dɪʃ/ 15
set-square /ˈset skweəʳ/ 56
settee /seˈtiː/ 14
seven /ˈsevən/ 107
seven (o'clock) /ˌsevən əˈklɒk/ 111
seventeen /ˌsevənˈtiːn/ 107
seventy /ˈsevənti/ 107
sew /səʊ/ 21
sewing /ˈsəʊɪŋ/ 94

sewing basket /ˈsəʊɪŋ ˌbɑːskɪt/ 52
sewing machine /ˈsəʊɪŋ məˌʃiːn/ 52, 94
sex /seks/ 6
shade /ʃeɪd/ 97
shake hands /ˌʃeɪk ˈhændz/ 37
shallow /ˈʃæləʊ/ 125
shalwar kameez /ˌʃælwɑːr kæˈmiːz/ 49
shampoo /ʃæmˈpuː/ 12, 39, 40
shapes /ʃeɪps/ 50
shark /ʃɑːk/ 104
shashlik /ˈʃæʃlɪk/ 65
shave /ʃeɪv/ 8
shaved hair /ˌʃeɪvd ˈheəʳ/ 36
shaving brush /ˈʃeɪvɪŋ brʌʃ/ 12
shaving gel /ˈʃeɪvɪŋ dʒel/ 12, 40
shears /ʃɪəz/ 19
sheep /ʃiːp/ 102
sheet /ʃiːt/ 13
sheet music /ˈʃiːt ˌmjuːzɪk/ 93
Sheffield /ˈʃefiːld/ 112
shelf /ʃelf/ 12
shell /ʃel/ 97
shelves /ʃelvz/ 58
shepherd's pie /ˌʃepədz ˈpaɪ/ 70
Shetland Islands /ˈʃetlənd ˌaɪləndz/ 112
shin /ʃɪn/ 34
ship /ʃɪp/ 78
shirt /ʃɜːt/ 48
shish kebab /ˌʃɪʃ kɪˈbæb/ 67
shoe shop /ˈʃuː ʃɒp/ 84
shoelace /ˈʃuːleɪs/ 50
shoes /ʃuːz/ 47
shop /ʃɒp/ 81
shopkeeper /ˈʃɒpˌkiːpəʳ/ 25
shopper /ˈʃɒpəʳ/ 62
shopping /ˈʃɒpɪŋ/ 62
shopping bag /ˈʃɒpɪŋ bæg/ 53, 62
short /ʃɔːt/ 36, 125
short hair /ˌʃ. ˈ./ 36
shorts /ʃɔːts/ 48
short-sleeved /ˌʃɔːt ˈsliːvd/ 50
shoulder /ˈʃəʊldəʳ/ 34
shoulder bag /ˈʃ.. ˌ./ 53
shoulder-length hair /ˌ.. . ˈ./ 36
shovel /ˈʃʌvəl/ 31
shower /ˈʃaʊəʳ/ 12
shower curtain /ˈʃaʊə ˌkɜːtn/ 12
shower gel /ˈʃaʊə dʒel/ 12
shrimp /ʃrɪmp/ 104
shutter /ˈʃʌtəʳ/ 9
shuttlecock /ˈʃʌtlkɒk/ 88
shy /ʃaɪ/ 124
side /saɪd/ 108
side salad /ˌsaɪd ˌsæləd/ 66
side table /ˈ. ˌ../ 15
side vegetables /ˈsaɪd ˌvedʒtəbəlz/ 66
sideburns /ˈsaɪdbɜːnz/ 36
sidelight /ˈsaɪdlaɪt/ 73
sieve /sɪv/ 11
sign a letter /ˌsaɪn ə ˈletəʳ/ 28
signpost /ˈsaɪnpəʊst/ 98
signs /saɪnz/ 75

Sikh /siːk/ 110
Sikh temple /ˌsiːk ˈtempəl/ 110
silk /sɪlk/ 52
silver /ˈsɪlvəʳ/ 53
sing /sɪŋ/ 37
singer /ˈsɪŋəʳ/ 93
single /ˈsɪŋgəl/ 6
single bed /ˌsɪŋgəl ˈbed/ 13
single parent /ˌsɪŋgəl ˈpeərənt/ 7
singlet /ˈsɪŋglət/ 49
sink /sɪŋk/ 10
sister /ˈsɪstəʳ/ 7
sisters-in-law /ˈsɪstəz ɪn lɔː/ 7
sit /sɪt/ 37
sitting room /ˈsɪtɪŋ ruːm/ 20
six /sɪks/ 107
six-pack /ˈsɪks pæk/ 68
sixteen /ˌsɪkˈstiːn/ 107
sixty /ˈsɪksti/ 107
skate /skeɪt/ 91
skateboard /ˈskeɪtbɔːd/ 55
skeleton /ˈskelɪtən/ 35
ski /skiː/ 91
ski boot /ˈskiː buːt/ 91
skier /ˈskiːəʳ/ 91
skip /skɪp/ 92
skipping rope /ˈskɪpɪŋ rəʊp/ 92
skirt /skɜːt/ 47, 48
skull /skʌl/ 35
sky /skaɪ/ 81
skydiver /ˈskaɪˌdaɪvəʳ/ 89
skydiving /ˈskaɪˌdaɪvɪŋ/ 89
skyline /ˈskaɪlaɪn/ 81
skyscraper /ˈskaɪˌskreɪpəʳ/ 81
sledge /sledʒ/ 91
sledgehammer /ˈsledʒˌhæməʳ/ 31
sledging /ˈsledʒɪŋ/ 91
sleep /sliːp/ 8
sleeping bag /ˈsliːpɪŋ bæg/ 98
sleeve /sliːv/ 50
slice /slaɪs/ 69
slide /slaɪd/ 55
slide projector /ˈslaɪd prəˌdʒektəʳ/ 123
slides /slaɪdz/ 123
slim /slɪm/ 36
sling /slɪŋ/ 44
slip /slɪp/ 47
slip road /ˈslɪp rəʊd/ 74
slippers /ˈslɪpəz/ 47
slippery road sign /ˌslɪpəri ˈrəʊd saɪn/ 75
Slovakia /sləʊˈvækiː/ 116
Slovenia /sləʊˈviːniə/ 116
slow /sləʊ/ 125
slug pellets /ˈslʌg ˌpeləts/ 19
small animals /ˌsmɔːl ˈænɪməlz/ 106
small intestine /ˌsmɔːl ɪnˈtestɪn/ 35
smile /smaɪl/ 37
smoke /sməʊk/ 85
smoked ham /ˌsməʊkt ˈhæm/ 64
smoked salmon /ˌsməʊkt ˈsæmən/ 65
smooth /smuːð/ 125
smoothie /ˈsmuːði/ 67
snail /sneɪl/ 106

snake /sneɪk/ 103
snapdragon /ˈsnæpˌdrægən/ 18
sneakers AmE /ˈsniːkəz/ 47
snorkel /ˈsnɔːkəl/ 90
snorkeller /ˈsnɔːkələr/ 90
snorkelling /ˈsnɔːkəlɪŋ/ 90
snout /snaʊt/ 104
snow /snəʊ/ 91
snowboard /ˈsnəʊbɔːd/ 91
snowmobile /ˈsnəʊməˌbiːl/ 91
snowmobiling /ˈsnəʊməˌbiːlɪŋ/ 91
snowy /ˈsnəʊi/ 118
soap /səʊp/ 12
soap dish /ˈsəʊp dɪʃ/ 12
soap dispenser /ˈsəʊp dɪˌspensəʳ/ 12
social worker /ˈsəʊʃəl ˌwɜːkəʳ/ 26
sociology /ˌsəʊsiˈɒlədʒi, ˌsəʊʃi-/ 57
socket /ˈsɒkɪt/ 17
socks /sɒks/ 48
sofa /ˈsəʊfə/ 14
soft /sɒft/ 125
soft top /ˈsɒft tɒp/ 73
soft toy /ˌsɒft ˈtɔɪ/ 16
software /ˈsɒftweəʳ/ 120
software engineer /ˈsɒftweər endʒɪˌnɪəʳ/ 26
solar system /ˈsəʊlə ˌsɪstəm/ 119
soldier /ˈsəʊldʒəʳ/ 23
sole /səʊl/ 50
solicitor /səˈlɪsɪtəʳ/ 33
son /sʌn/ 7
son-in-law /ˈsʌn ɪn lɔː/ 7
sore throat /ˌsɔː ˈθrəʊt/ 41
soup /suːp/ 62
soup and bread roll /ˌsuːp ən bred ˈrəʊl/ 70
soup spoon /ˈsuːp spuːn/ 15
South America /ˌsaʊθ əˈmerɪkə/ 114
South Carolina /ˌsaʊθ kærəˈlaɪnə/ 113
South Dakota /ˌsaʊθ dəˈkəʊtə/ 113
space shuttle /ˈspeɪs ˌʃʌtl/ 119
space suit /ˈspeɪs suːt/ 119
spade /speɪd/ 19, 97
spaghetti bolognese /spəˌgeti bɒləˈneɪz/ 70
Spain /speɪn/ 116
Spanish /ˈspænɪʃ/ 57
speak /spiːk/ 37
speaker /ˈspiːkəʳ/ 122
speakers /ˈspiːkəz/ 120
Special Delivery™ /ˌspeʃəl dɪˈlɪvəri/ 82
speed skater /ˈspiːd ˌskeɪtəʳ/ 91
speed skating /ˈspiːd ˌskeɪtɪŋ/ 91
speedometer /spɪˈdɒmɪtəʳ/ 73
sphere /sfɪəʳ/ 108
spice rack /ˈspaɪs ræk/ 10
spices /ˈspaɪsɪz/ 10
spider /ˈspaɪdəʳ/ 106
spinach /ˈspɪnɪdʒ, -ɪtʃ/ 59
spine /spaɪn/ 35

water skier /ˈ.. ˌ../ **90**
water skiing /ˈwɔːtə ˌskiːɪŋ/ **90**
water the plants /ˈ.. . ˈ./ **19**
watercress /ˈwɔːtəkres/ **59**
waterfall /ˈwɔːtəfɔːl/ **117**
watering can /ˈwɔːtərɪŋ ˌkæn/ **19**
watermelon /ˈwɔːtəˌmelən/ **61**
wave /weɪv/ **37, 97**
wavy hair /ˌweɪvi ˈheəʳ/ **36**
weather /ˈweðəʳ/ **118**
web /web/ **106**
web address /ˈweb əˌdres‖ˌædres/ **121**
web browser /ˈweb ˌbrauzəʳ/ **121**
web-cam /ˈweb kæm/ **120**
website /ˈwebsaɪt/ **121**
Wednesday /ˈwenzdeɪ/ **109**
weed the flowerbed /ˌwiːd ðə ˈflauəbed/ **19**
weigh /weɪ/ **69**
weights /weɪts/ **92**
wellies /ˈweliz/ **47**
wellingtons /ˈwelɪŋtənz/ **47**
Welsh National Assembly /ˌwelʃ ˌnæʃənəl əˈsembli/ **100**
West Virginia /ˌwest vəˈdʒɪniə/ **113**
wet /wet/ **125**
wet suit /ˈ. ./ **90**
whale /weɪl/ **104**

wheel /wiːl/ **73, 89**
wheelbarrow /ˈwiːlˌbærəu/ **19, 31**
wheelchair /ˈwiːltʃeəʳ/ **44**
whisk /wɪsk/ **11**
whiskers /ˈwɪskəz/ **101**
white /waɪt/ **51**
white bread /ˌ. ˈ./ **64**
white wine /ˌwaɪt ˈwaɪn/ **63, 66**
whiteboard /ˈwaɪtbɔːd/ **56**
whiteboard marker /ˈwaɪtbɔːd ˌmɑːkəʳ/ **56**
white-collar worker /ˌ. ˈ.. ˌ../ **25**
whole trout /ˌhəul ˈtraut/ **64**
wholemeal bread /ˌhəulmiːl ˈbred/ **64**
wicket /ˈwɪkɪt/ **86**
wicket keeper /ˈwɪkɪt ˌkiːpəʳ/ **86**
wide /waɪd/ **50, 125**
widow /ˈwɪdəu/ **6**
widower /ˈwɪdəuəʳ/ **6**
width /wɪdθ/ **108**
wife /waɪf/ **7**
wildlife park /ˈwaɪldlaɪf ˌpɑːk/ **99**
windbreak /ˈwɪndbreɪk/ **97**
window /ˈwɪndəu/ **9, 14, 20, 77, 120**
window cleaner /ˈwɪndəu ˌkliːnəʳ/ **23**

window seat /ˈwɪndəu siːt/ **77**
windscreen wiper /ˈwɪndskriːn ˌwaɪpəʳ/ **73**
wind-surfer /ˈwɪnd ˌsɜːfəʳ/ **90**
windy /ˈwɪndi/ **118**
wine glass /ˈwaɪn glɑːs/ **15**
wine list /waɪn lɪst/ **65**
wing /wɪŋ/ **73, 77**
wing mirror /ˈwɪŋ ˌmɪrəʳ/ **73**
wings /wɪŋz/ **105**
winter /ˈwɪntəʳ/ **118**
Wisconsin /wɪˈskɒnsɪn/ **113**
withdrawal slip /wɪðˈdrɔːəl slɪp/ **79**
witness /ˈwɪtnɪs/ **33**
wok /wɒk/ **11**
woman /ˈwumən/ **6**
wood /wud/ **117**
woodwind /ˈwud wɪnd/ **96**
woodworking /ˈwudˌwɜːkɪŋ/ **94**
wool /wul/ **52**
word processor /wɜːd ˈprəusesəʳ/ **120**
work station /ˈwɜːk ˌsteɪʃən/ **30**
workbench /ˈwɜːkbentʃ/ **29**
worker /ˈwɜːkəʳ/ **30**
work-surface /ˈwɜːk ˌsɜːfɪs/ **10**
worktop /ˈwɜːktɒp/ **10**
world wide web /ˌwɜːld waɪd ˈweb/ **121**

wrapping paper /ˈræpɪŋ ˌpeɪpəʳ/ **83**
wrench /rentʃ/ **29**
wrestler /ˈresləʳ/ **88**
wrestling /ˈreslɪŋ/ **88**
wrist /rɪst/ **34**
write /raɪt/ **38**
write a memo /ˌraɪt ə ˈmeməu/ **28**
writing paper /ˈraɪtɪŋ ˌpeɪpəʳ/ **83**
Wyoming /waɪˈəumɪŋ/ **113**
X-ray /ˈeks reɪ/ **43**
X-ray scanner /ˈeks reɪ ˌskænəʳ/ **76**
X-rays /ˈeks reɪz/ **44**
xylophone /ˈzaɪləfəun/ **96**
yacht /jɒt/ **78, 90**
yam /jæm/ **60**
yard AmE /jɑːd/ **9**
yellow /ˈjeləu/ **51**
yellow card /ˌ.. ˈ./ **86**
yoghurt / yogurt /ˈjɒgət/ **62**
York /jɔːk/ **112**
zebra /ˈzebrə, ˈziː-/ **103**
zebra crossing /ˌzebrə ˈkrɒsɪŋ/ **74, 80**
zero /ˈzɪərəu/ **107**
zip /zɪp/ **50**
zoo /zuː/ **99**

1   PEOPLE

1.1   Use the information about Denzel Washington to complete the application form.

Denzel Washington   28/12/1954   994-9872
1106 Hollywood Drive, Los Angeles   Actor   Male
CA 98554   Married   American
Pauletta Pearson   Four children   Mount Vernon, New York

1 First name	_Denzel_	
2 Surname		
3 Sex		
4 Occupation		
5 Address		
6 Postcode		

7 Telephone number	
8 Nationality	
9 Date of birth	
10 Place of birth	
11 Marital status	
12 Husband's / wife's name	
13 Number of children	

1.2   Put the male and female words in the correct column.

aunt, father, granddaughter, grandmother, half-sister, mother-in-law, nephew, sister, stepfather, stepson

	Male	**Female**		**Male**	**Female**
Example	_widower_	_widow_			
1	brother		**6**		stepdaughter
2		mother	**7**	father-in-law	
3	uncle		**8**	half-brother	
4	grandfather		**9**	grandson	
5		niece	**10**	stepmother	

1.3   The family on page 7 have some other relatives. Look at their family tree again and complete the sentences below.

aunt, brother-in-law, cousin, grandmother, mother-in-law, nephew, ~~sister-in-law~~, uncle

Example Ann Elliot has a sister, Fiona. Fiona is Robert's ___sister-in-law___.

1 Ann Elliot has a sister, Fiona. Fiona is Sue and Tim's _____.
2 Robert Elliot has a brother, Jim. Jim is Ann's _____ and Sue and Tim's _____.
3 Elaina's mother, Julia, is Tim's _____ and Tessa and Chris's _____.
4 Elaina has a brother, Thomas. His son, Henry, is Tessa and Chris's _____. Henry is Elaina's _____.

1.4   What do you do in the morning? Write these activities in the order you do them.

brush your teeth	**1**	_wake up_
dry yourself	**2**	
eat breakfast	**3**	
get dressed	**4**	
get up	**5**	
have a shower	**6**	
~~wake up~~	**7**	

2   HOUSING

**2.1   Look at the ground floor plan.
Where can you find these objects?
Write the correct numbers in each room.**

> 1 armchair, 2 bin, 3 bookcase,
> 4 broom, 5 coffee table,
> 6 cushion, 7 dining table,
> 8 dishwasher, 9 double oven,
> 10 freezer, 11 fridge / refrigerator,
> 12 ironing board, 13 napkin ring,
> 14 place mat, 15 scrubbing brush,
> 16 side table, 17 sofa,
> 18 vacuum cleaner, 19 vase,
> 20 washing machine

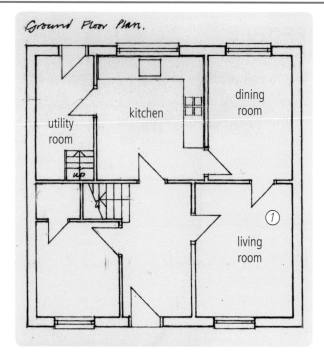

**2.2   Find the words for these objects in the bathroom.
Put the correct number next to the word.**

soap dispenser	8
shaving brush	
toothbrush holder	
shaving gel	
soap	
razor	
toothbrush	
mug	
toothpaste	
soap dish	

2.3   What do you need to do these things? Write one object from the box below next to each activity.

> alarm clock, bath towel, cafetière, cake tin, kettle, mop, tea towel, tumbler dryer, watering can

Example make coffee   _cafetière_

1 dry the dishes   ....

2 dry yourself   ....

3 boil water   ....

4 water the plants   ....

5 make a cake   ....

6 wake up   ....

7 dry clothes   ....

8 wash the floor   ....

2.4   Complete the words and write them below. All these things go on the dining room table.

Example   f _o_ rk   _fork_

1 sp___on   ....

2 w___ne glas___   ....

3 des___ertspo___n   ....

4 ser___iette   ....

5 so___p spo___n   ....

6 s___lt   ....

7 kn___fe   ....

8 p___pper   ....

9 t___asp___on   ....

3 WORK / OCCUPATIONS

3.1 Where can you find these people or things? Put these words in the correct box.

bar, barrister, bulldozer, cement, chambermaid, conveyer belt, electric drill, ~~fax machine~~, foreman, forklift, guard, photocopier, sand saw, scaffolding, stapler, twin room, witness, wrench

Office	Workshop	Factory	Construction site	Hotel	Court
fax machine					

3.2 What do these people do? Write the jobs under the correct picture.

artist, bricklayer, butcher, ~~carpenter~~, hairdresser, judge, midwife, optician, photographer, security guard

1 *carpenter* 2 .... 3 .... 4 .... 5 ....

6 .... 7 .... 8 .... 9 .... 10 ....

3.3 Fill in the letters to complete the words. All of these phrases are activities in the office.

n	**o**	*t*	*e*	appointments
	f			papers
	f			refreshments
	i			a letter
c				a document
	e			an e-mail

EXERCISES

4 THE BODY

4.1 Write a sentence for the actions in these pictures.

Example *She is hugging her friend.*

1 ....
2 ....
3 ....
4 ....

5 ....
6 ....
7 ....
8 ....

4.2 Complete these sentences with the words in the box.

bones, brain, ears, eyes, fingers, head, nails, nose, teeth, ~~toes~~

Example A foot has five ____toes____ .

1 A hand has five ....
2 You see with your ....
3 You hear with your ....
4 You smell with your ....
5 You type with your ....

6 You wear a hat on your ....
7 An adult has 32 ....
8 Your skeleton has many ....
9 Your .... controls your body.

4.3 Find the missing letters to make a new word. You can find these things at the hairdresser's and the beauty salon.

Word	Missing letter
1 lipsti___k	___c___
2 styling m___usse	....
3 nail sci___sors	....
4 ___ascara	....
5 hairdry___r	....

Word	Missing letter
6 ho___ wax	....
7 fac___al	....
8 ___ologne	....
9 after___have	....
New word	....

5 HEALTH

5.1 **What medical specialist do you need to see for these health problems below?**
Match the words in the box with the problems.

> chiropodist, dentist, dermatologist, ~~general practitioner~~, osteopath, physiotherapist

1 cough _general practitioner_ **2** backache .... **3** rash ....

4 weak muscles .... **5** swollen foot .... **6** toothache ....

5.2 **Match these ailments to the parts of body.**
Write the correct number next to the word.

Example black eye   `4`

broken arm ☐
headache ☐
nose bleed ☐
sprained ankle ☐
sore throat ☐
stomach ache ☐

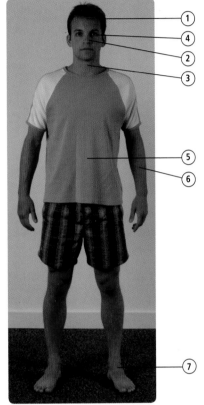

5.3 **What kind of medicine are these? Unscramble the letters.**

Example eey rdpos   _eye drops_

1 inillkresap .... **5** ilp malb ....
2 eugaz .... **6** restlap ....
3 sustise .... **7** merca ....
4 sryap ....

5.4 **Write these words in the correct boxes.**

> anaesthetist, basin, dentures, drill, ~~examination couch~~, height chart, plaque, scales, scalpel, stethoscope, surgeon, surgical gloves

In the doctor's surgery	In the operating theatre	In the dental surgery
examination couch		

EXERCISES

6 FOOD

6.1 **Write the names of these fruit and vegetables under the correct picture.**

apricot, cherry, chilli pepper, ~~cucumber~~, garlic, lychee, pak choi, pomegranate, radish, watermelon

1 _cucumber_   2 ....   3 ....   4 ....   5 ....

6 ....   7 ....   8 ....   9 ....   10 ....

6.2 **Ten of the items are listed in the wrong category. Write the dishes and drinks in the correct part of the menu.**

Starters	Main courses	Desserts	Drinks
lasagne	roast beef with Yorkshire pudding	pizza	fizzy mineral water
borscht	tomato soup	cheesecake	panna cotta
~~orange juice~~	koftas	tiramisu	cola
melon and parma ham	ice cream	still mineral water	smoked salmon
	moussaka	apple pie	strawberry smoothie
	tea		coffee
	fajitas		fillet of sole
			orange juice

6.3 **Complete the conversations with the words in the box.**

baguette, butter, cheese, condiments, delicatessen, dog food, dry goods, ~~frozen foods~~, meat, washing powder, wholemeal bread

Example **A** I would like to buy fish fingers and pizza.   **B** Go to the _frozen foods_ section.

1 **A** I would like to buy .... and ....   **B** Go to the dairy products section.

2 **A** I would like to buy herbs and spices.   **B** Go to the .... section.

3 **A** I would like to buy rice and flour.   **B** Go to the .... section.

4 **A** I would like to buy .... and ....   **B** Go to the household products section.

5 **A** I would like to buy salami and smoked ham.   **B** Go to the .... counter.

6 **A** I would like to buy .... and a ....   **B** Go to the bakery.

7 **A** I would like to buy lamb chops and steak.   **B** Go to the .... counter.

7 TRANSPORT

7.1 Put these words in the correct category.

> carriage, cat's eye, check-in desk, customs, duty-free shop, ferry, flyover, inside lane, liner, metal detector, platform, road sign, rowing boat, runway, sailing ship, track, traffic lights, train

At the railway station	On the road	At the airport	Water transport
carriage			

7.2 Write the number of the car parts on the pictures.

1 brake light	**4** gear lever	**7** wheel	**10** speedometer
2 exhaust pipe	**5** rear windscreen	**8** boot	**11** fuel gauge
3 wing mirror	**6** sidelight	**9** bonnet	**12** headlight

7.3 What do these signs mean? Match the signs to their meanings. Number the words.

cyclists only	6	give way		level crossing		no overtaking	
no through road		no U-turn		roadworks ahead		no right turn	
roundabout		steep hill		slippery road		stop	

1   2   3

4   5   6

7   8   9

10   11   12

7.4 Fill in the letters to complete the transport words.

_r_	_e_	**t**	_u_	_r_	_n_	ticket
		r				car
		a				driver
		n			mirror	
		s			hour	
		p				carrier
		o				officer
		r				scanner
		t				sign

EXERCISES

8 COMMUNITY

8.1 Complete these sentences with the words in the box.

> bank, cashpoint, chequebook, coins, euro, financial adviser, notes, pin number, ~~pounds~~

Example I spend thirty ___*pounds*___ on food every day.

1   I have ten pound _____ I don't have any _____.
2   The currency in many European countries is called the _____.
3   My dad works as a _____ in a _____.
4   I never pay by cheque. I don't have a _____.
5   I can't use my _____ card. I forgot my _____.

8.2 These are some of the things you can buy at the newsagent's. Use the words below to label them.

> ~~bag of sweets~~
> bar of chocolate
> box of chocolates,
> chewing gum
> fudge
> lollipop
> magazine
> mints
> packet of crisps
> paperback

Example

| bag of sweets |

| 2 |

| 3 |

| 6 |

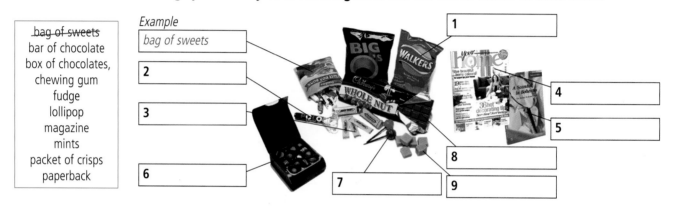

| 1 |

| 4 |

| 5 |

| 8 |

| 7 | | 9 |

8.3 Where do you need to go? Write the name of the place to answer each question.

> book shop, electronics shop, jeweller's, ~~newsagent's~~, optician's, post office, travel agency

Example I want to buy a newspaper.   The ___*newsagent's*___

1   I would like some stamps.   The _____
2   I want to buy a new fridge.   The _____
3   I want to buy earrings for my sister. The _____
4   I want to go on holiday.   The _____
5   I would like to buy a book.   The _____
6   I would like new glasses.   The _____

8.4 Find the names of eight things in the city life word puzzle.

O	T	S	T	R	E	E	T	B	C	N
S	N	G	R	K	B	A	U	L	Q	R
H	F	T	A	A	N	L	Z	C	K	B
L	B	C	F	G	I	N	I	A	E	P
B	N	R	F	B	O	L	L	A	R	D
E	Z	I	I	S	C	N	I	J	B	V
G	X	V	C	D	V	C	T	N	A	B
T	L	E	V	E	G	F	L	A	G	U
A	P	R	B	N	A	E	K	E	C	S

9 SPORTS

9.1 Match the words to the sports.

1 bat [b]   **2** penalty spot [ ]   **3** posts [ ]   **4** ring [ ]   **5** jockey [ ]   **6** racket [ ]

7 shuttlecock [ ]   **8** bow [ ]   **9** helmet [ ]   **10** leotard [ ]   **11** wet suit [ ]   **12** paddle [ ]

a rugby   **b** cricket   **c** boxing   **d** football   **e** tennis   **f** horse racing

g gymnastics   **h** scuba diving   **i** badminton   **j** canoeing   **k** archery   **l** rollerblading

Example **1** __bat__ goes with __b cricket__

2 ....   **3** ....   **4** ....   **5** ....

6 ....   **7** ....   **8** ....   **9** ....

10 ....   **11** ....   **12** ....

9.2 What are these sports? Label the pictures.

climbing, cycling, diving, figure skating, judo, parachuting, rowing, water skiing

1 __water skiing__

2 ....

3 ....

4 ....

5 ....

6 ....

7 ....

8 ....

9.3 Put these words in the correct columns. You can use some of the words more than once.

bails, ball (2), bat, batsman, bowler, boxer, boxing, club, course, court, cricket, fielder, figure skater, figure skates, figure skating, football, football boots, footballer, gloves, goalie, goggles, golf, golf ball, golfer, ice rink, net (2), pitch (2), pool, racket, ring, stump, swimmer, swimming, swimming cap, swimming costume, tennis, tennis ball, tennis player, trunks, wicket keeper

Sport	Place	Equipment	Players
cricket	pitch	bat, ball, bails, stump	batsman, bowler, fielder, wicket keeper

EXERCISES

10 RECREATION

10.1 What hobbies do you think of when you see these things? Write these words under the correct pictures.

astronomy, bird-watching, playing card games, playing chess, cookery, ~~doing crosswords~~, stamp collecting, doing sudoku puzzles

1 _doing crosswords_   2 ....   3 ....   4 ....

5 ....   6 ....   7 ....   8 ....

10.2 What instruments are these? Unscramble the letters.

Example tpurtem ___trumpet___

1 lufet ....
2 badsroeyk ....
3 myalbc ....
4 olecl ....
5 nosbosa ....

6 etinracl ....
7 lnlovi ....
8 booe ....
9 corerrde ....
10 enphoxloy ....

11 onidorcac ....
12 lococip ....
13 ilaov ....
14 umrd ....

10.3 Complete the text with the words in the box.

band, ballerina, ~~ballet~~, classical, concerts, keyboard, piano

When I was five, I took ___ballet___ classes. I wanted to become a famous .... but I wasn't very good.
Then I learned to play the .... I liked listening to .... music. As a teenager, I started going to rock
.... with my friends. I played the .... in the school ....

10.4 Put the words in the box in the correct columns.

~~beach towel~~, bikini, camping stove, campsite, nature reserve, pier, rucksack, sand, shell, signpost, sleeping bag, sunscreen

Things you take to the beach	Things you find at the beach	Things you take to the countryside	Things you find in the country
beach towel	....	....	....
....	....	....	....
....	....	....	....

10.5 Here are some places to visit. Write the missing words from the box to complete the phrases.

Cathedral, garden, home, Lords, Palace, park, tower

Example theme ___park___

1 church ....
5 Canterbury ....

2 stately ....
6 House of ....

3 botanical ....
7 safari ....

4 Buckingham ....

11 ANIMALS

11.1 Write the names of these animals under the correct picture.

badger, bear, buffalo, chick, duck, foal, giraffe, ~~rabbit~~, tiger

1 _rabbit_   2 ....   3 ....   4 ....   5 ....

6 ....   7 ....   8 ....   9 ....   10 ....

11.2 Match these animals with their babies.

calf, duckling, foal, gosling, ~~kid~~, kitten, lamb, piglet, puppy

Example goat   _kid_

1 cow ....   2 sheep ....   3 goose ....   4 duck ....
5 horse ....   6 pig ....   7 cat ....   8 dog ....

11.3 Write the name of each group of animals. Cross out the animal that does not belong there.

birds, fish, insects, sea animals, ~~wild animals~~

1 _wild animals_	2	3	4	5
elephant	shark	dolphin	robin	wasp
giraffe	trout	crocodile	ladybird	cockroach
~~cockerel~~	eel	walrus	penguin	snail
rhinoceros	gorilla	crab	swallow	spider
kangaroo	sunfish	whale	crane	caterpillar

11.4 Answer these questions about animals.

Example Do tigers eat meat?   _Yes, they do._

1 Do cows provide milk?   ....
2 Do cats lay eggs?   ....
3 Can penguins fly?   ....
4 Can owls see well at night?   ....
5 Do parrots have long legs?   ....

6 Can seals live under water?   ....
7 Do peacocks have wings?   ....
8 Do moles live in the sea?   ....
9 Do spiders have ears?   ....

12 NUMBERS, HOLIDAYS, MAPS

12.1 Look at these numbers and fill in the missing words.

101
1,000
10,000
100,000
1,000,000

hundred (2), million, thousand (2)

101   one _hundred_ and one   **1,000** one ....   **10,000** ten ....

100,000 one .... thousand   **1,000,000** one ....

12.2 Look at the shapes and label the different parts. Use the words in the box.

apex, base, corner, depth, edge, face, height, hypotenuse, right angle, top

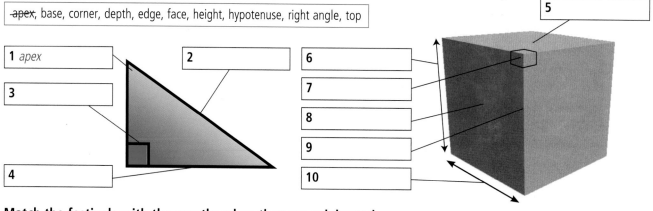

1 apex

2

3

4

5

6

7

8

9

10

12.3 Match the festivals with the months when they are celebrated.

Example **1** Easter Day [b]   **2** Halloween [ ]   **3** Christmas Day [ ]   **4** Bonfire Night [ ]   **5** Diwali [ ]   **6** St Valentine's Day [ ]

a   December   **b**   March or April   **c**   October   **d**   February   **e**   October or November   **f**   November

12.4 Look at the clocks and complete the sentences.

Example I wake up at _seven o'clock_ in the morning.   **3** I eat breakfast at ....

1 I get up at ....   **4** At ...., I brush my teeth.

2 At ...., I have a shower.   **5** I go to work at ....

12.5 Write these countries under the correct continent.

Australia, Brazil, Bulgaria, Canada, Chile, China, Cuba, Denmark, Ghana, Laos, Libya, Mali, Mexico, New Zealand, Pakistan, Papua New Guinea, Peru, Spain

Asia	Africa	North America	South America	Europe	Australia
China					

13 THE ENVIRONMENT

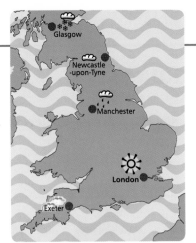

13.1 Write the weather for each of these places.

Example: In Exeter it is ___foggy___.

1 In London it is _____
2 In Manchester it is _____
3 In Newcastle it is _____
4 In Glasgow it is _____

13.2 Look at the pictures and fill in the letters to complete the words.

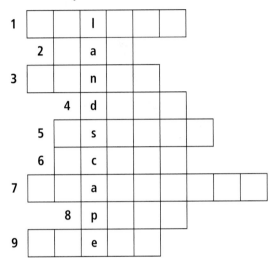

			l			
	2		a			
3			n			
		4	d			
5			s			
6			c			
7			a			
		8	p			
9			e			

13.3 Look at the pictures and correct the mistakes. Use the words in the box. Write the correct sentence.

hot, lightning, rainy, spring, sunny, windy, winter

Example

It is summer. It is cold and rainy.
___It is summer. It is hot and sunny.___

It is spring. It is cold and snowy.
1 _____

It is winter. It is warm and sunny.
2 _____

You see a rainbow before you hear thunder.
3 _____

I take an umbrella when it is foggy.
4 _____

It is very stormy today.
5 _____

13.4 Write the names of the planets in the correct order from the nearest to the furthest from the sun.

Mercury	Saturn	Pluto
Earth	Venus	Neptune
Jupiter	Mars	Uranus

1 _____   4 _____   7 _____
2 _____   5 _____   8 _____
3 _____   6 _____   9 _____

14 EXPRESSING ONESELF

14.1 **Look at the pictures. How does the woman feel in each one? Write the adjectives under the correct picture.**

angry, annoyed, ecstatic, furious, happy, nervous, ~~sad~~, shy, surprised, suspicious

1 _sad_   2 ....   3 ....   4 ....   5 ....

14.2 **Match the opposites.**

1 neat [f]   **2** heavy [ ]   **3** long [ ]   **4** thin [ ]   **5** empty [ ]   **6** slow [ ]   **7** wide [ ]   **8** shallow [ ]   **9** expensive [ ]

a cheap   **b** deep   **c** fast   **d** full   **e** light   **f** messy   **g** narrow   **h** short   **i** thick

14.3 **Answer these questions using the opposite preposition.**

from, inside, down, under, off

Example Is he standing in front of her?   _No, behind her._

1 Is she sitting on top of the table?
No, ...

2 Is he outside the flat?
No, ...

3 Is the light on?
No, it's ....

4 Is he walking towards the station?
No, ...

5 Is he going up the stairs?
No, ...

14.4 **What is the girl doing in these pictures? Use these prepositions to describe her.**

against, into, off, ~~onto~~, out of, through

Example

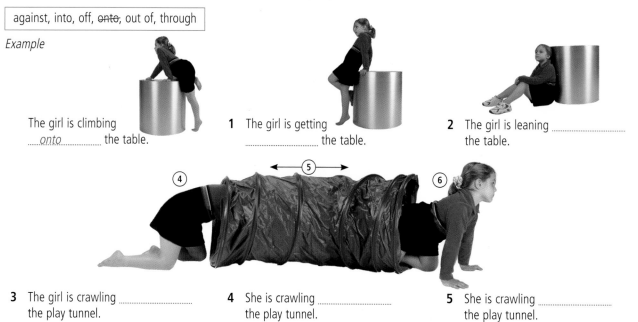

The girl is climbing _onto_ the table.

1 The girl is getting .... the table.

2 The girl is leaning .... the table.

3 The girl is crawling .... the play tunnel.

4 She is crawling .... the play tunnel.

5 She is crawling .... the play tunnel.

1 PEOPLE

1.1
2 Washington
3 Male
4 actor
5 1106 Hollywood Drive, Los Angeles
6 CA 98554
7 994-9872
8 American
9 21/12/1954
10 Mount Vernon, New York
11 married
12 Pauletta Pearson
13 four

1.2
1 sister
2 father
3 aunt
4 grandmother
5 nephew
6 stepson
7 mother-in-law
8 half-sister
9 granddaughter
10 stepfather

1.3
1 aunt
2 brother-in-law & uncle
3 mother-in-law & grandmother
4 cousin & nephew

1.4
2 have a shower
3 dry yourself
4 get dressed
5 eat breakfast
6 brush your teeth

2 HOUSING

2.1
utility room
4, 12, 18, 20
kitchen
2, 8, 9, 10, 11
dining room
7, 13, 14, 16
living room
3, 5, 6, 13, 15, 17

2.2
1 mug
2 soap dish
3 toothbrush
4 toothbrush holder
5 razor
6 shaving gel
7 shaving brush
8 soap dispenser
9 soap

2.3
2 tea towel
3 bath towel
4 kettle
5 watering can
6 cake tin
7 alarm clock
8 tumble dryer
9 mop

2.4
1 spoon
2 wine glass
3 dessertspoon
4 serviette
5 knife
6 soup spoon
7 salt
8 pepper
9 teaspoon

3 WORK / OCCUPATIONS

3.1
office
fax machine
photocopier
stapler
workshop
electric drill
sand saw
wrench
factory
conveyer belt
foreman
forklift
construction site
bulldozer
cement
scaffolding
hotel
bar
chambermaid
twin room
court
barrister
guard
witness

3.2
2 butcher
3 bricklayer
4 optician
5 judge
6 artist
7 photographer
8 midwife
9 security guard
10 hairdresser

3.3
note appointments
file papers
offer refreshments
sign a letter
photocopy a document
send an e-mail

4 THE BODY

4.1
1 She is waving.
2 She is frowning.
3 He is pushing a wheelbarrow.
4 She is clapping her hands.
5 She is filling the kettle.
6 She is pouring the water.
7 He is breaking the biscuit.
8 She is stirring the coffee.

4.2
1 nails
2 eyes
3 ears
4 nose
5 fingers
6 head
7 teeth
8 bones
9 brain

4.3
1 c
2 o
3 s
4 m
5 e
6 t
7 i
8 c
9 s
new word: cosmetics

5 HEALTH

5.1
2 osteopath
3 dermatologist
4 physiotherapist
5 chiropodist
6 dentist

5.2
1 headache
2 nose bleed
3 sore throat
4 stomach ache
5 broken arm
6 sprained ankle

5.3
1 painkillers
2 gauze
3 tissues
4 spray
5 lip balm
6 plaster
7 cream

5.4
In the doctor's surgery
examination couch
height chart
scales
stethoscope
In the operating surgery
anaesthetist
scalpel
surgeon
surgical gloves
In the dental surgery
basin
dentures
drill
plaque

6 FOOD

6.1
2 chilli pepper
3 watermelon
4 pomegranate
5 garlic
6 radish
7 pak choi
8 apricot
9 lychee

6.2
Starters
lasagne
borscht
melon and parma ham
tomato soup
smoked salmon
Main courses
roast beef and Yorkshire pudding
koftas
moussaka
fajitas
pizza
fillet of sole
Desserts
cheesecake
tiramisu
apple pie
panna cotta
Drinks
fizzy mineral water
cola
strawberry smoothie
coffee
orange juice
tea
still mineral water

6.3
1 cheese & butter
2 condiments
3 dry goods
4 dog food & washing powder
5 delicatessen
6 wholemeal bread & baguette
7 meat

7 TRANSPORT

7.1
At the railway station
carriage
platform
track
train
On the road
cat's eyes
flyover
inside lane
road sign
traffic lights
At the airport
check-in desk
duty-free shop
metal detector
runway
Water transport
ferry
liner
rowing boat
sailing ship

7.2
1 brake light
2 exhaust pipe
3 wing mirror
4 gear
5 rear windscreen
6 sidelight
7 wheel
8 boot
9 bonnet
11 fuel gauge
12 headlight

7.3
1 give way
2 no U-turn
3 no overtaking
4 steep hill
5 no through road
7 no right turn
8 slippery road
9 roadworks ahead
10 roundabout
11 level crossing
12 stop

7.4
sports car
taxi driver
wing mirror
rush hour
people carrier
customs officer
X-ray scanner
stop sign

8 COMMUNITY

8.1
1. notes & coins
2. euro
3. financial adviser & bank
4. chequebook
5. cashpoint & pin number

8.2
1. packet of crisps
2. mints
3. chewing gum
4. magazine
5. paperback
6. box of chocolates
7. lollipop
8. bar of chocolate
9. fudge

8.3
1. post office
2. electronics shop
3. jeweller's
4. travel agency
5. book shop
6. optician's

8.4
The eight words to find are
Across
STREET
BOLLARD
FLAG
Down
TRAFFIC
KERB
BUS
Diagonal
RAILINGS
BRIDGE

9 SPORTS

9.1
2. d
3. a
4. c
5. f
6. e
7. i
8. k
9. l
10. g
11. h
12. j

9.2
2. figure skating
3. parachuting
4. rowing
5. cycling
6. judo
7. diving
8. climbing

9.3

Sport	Place	Equipment	Players
football	pitch	ball, football boots, net	footballer, goalie
golf	course	club, golf ball	golfer
boxing	ring	gloves	boxer
tennis	court	racket, tennis ball, net	tennis player
swimming	pool	goggles, swimming costume, swimming cap, trunks	swimmer
figure skating	ice rink	figure skates	figure skater

10 RECREATION

10.1
1. playing card games
2. stamp collecting
3. bird-watching
4. astronomy
5. playing chess
6. doing sudoku puzzles
7. cookery

10.2
1. flute
2. keyboard
3. cymbal
4. cello
5. bassoon
6. clarinet
7. violin
8. oboe
9. recorder
10. xylophone
11. accordion
12. piccolo
13. viola
14. drum

10.3
When I was five, I took **ballet** classes. I wanted to become a famous **ballerina** but I wasn't very good. Then I learned to play the **piano**. I liked listening to **classical** music. As a teenager, I started going to rock **concerts** with my friends. I played the **keyboard** in the school **band**.

10.4
Things you take to the beach
beach towel
bikini
sunscreen
Things you find at the beach
pier
sand
shell
Things you take to the countryside
camping stove
rucksack
sleeping bag
Things you find in the country
campsite
nature reserve
signpost

10.5
1. tower
2. home
3. garden
4. Palace
5. Cathedral
6. Lords
7. park

11 ANIMALS

11.1
2. chick
3. duck
4. foal
5. tiger
6. bear
7. buffalo
8. badger
9. deer
10. giraffe

11.2
1. calf
2. lamb
3. gosling
4. duckling
5. foal
6. piglet
7. kitten
8. puppy

11.3
1. wild animals
   ~~cockerel~~
2. fish
   ~~gorilla~~
3. sea animals
   ~~crocodile~~
4. birds
   ~~ladybird~~
5. insects
   ~~snail~~

11.4
1. Yes, they do.
2. No, they don't.
3. No, they can't.
4. Yes, they can.
5. No, they don't.
6. Yes, they can.
7. Yes, they do.
8. No, they don't.
9. No, they don't.

12 NUMBERS, HOLIDAYS, MAPS

12.1
1,000 one thousand
10,000 ten thousand
100,000 one hundred thousand
1,000,000 one million

12.2
2. hypotenuse
3. right angle
4. base
5. top
6. height
7. corner
8. face
9. edge
10. depth

12.3
2 c, 3 a, 4 f, 5 e, 6 d

12.4
1. five past seven
2. ten past seven
3. seven thirty
4. ten to eight
5. eight o'clock

12.5
Asia
China
Laos
Pakistan
Africa
Ghana
Libya
Mali
North America
Canada
Cuba
Mexico
South America
Brazil
Chile
Peru

Europe
Bulgaria
Denmark
Spain
Australia
Australia
New Zealand
Papua New Guinea

13 THE ENVIRONMENT

13.1
1. In London it is sunny.
2. In Manchester it is cloudy and rainy.
3. In Newcastle it is cloudy.
4. In Glasgow it is snowy and cloudy.

13.2
1. valley
2. dam
3. canal
4. dune
5. island
6. acorn
7. coastline
8. peak
9. field

13.3
1. It is **winter**. It is cold and snowy.
2. It is **spring**. It is warm and sunny.
3. You see **lightning** before you hear thunder.
4. I take an umbrella when it is **rainy**.
5. It is very **windy** today.

13.4
1. Mercury
2. Venus
3. Earth
4. Mars
5. Jupiter
6. Saturn
7. Uranus
8. Neptune
9. Pluto

14 EXPRESSING ONESELF

14.1
2. ecstatic
3. furious
4. nervous
5. shy

14.2
2 e, 3 h, 4 l, 5 d, 6 c, 7 g, 8 b, 9 a

14.3
1. No, under the table.
2. No, inside the flat.
3. No, it's off.
4. No, away from the station.
5. No, down the stairs.

14.4
1. off
2. against
3. into
4. through
5. out of

PHOTO CREDITS

The Publishers would like to thank the following for their kind permission to reproduce their photographs:

Key: b bottom; c centre; l left; r right; t top

Alamy Images: Ange 122/6, Blend Images 32/9, British Retail Photography 84/14, BWAC Images 62/6, Camera lucida environment 55/3, Judith Collins 122/11, Louise Batalla Duran 109/10, 110/6, Elizabeth Whiting & Associates 120/8, Flashpoint Pictures / Ian Miles 57/18, S Forster 109/11, Stuart Forster 26/18, Sally and Richard Greenhill 54/2, Haydn Hansell 110/3, Jeremy Hoare 110/13, David Hoffman 24/12, 33/2, Horizon International Images Ltd 26/17, Image State 24/5, Janine Wiedel Photography 44/4, Lenscap 122/9, mainpicture 55/9, Mediacolor's 6/23l, Keith Morris 24/13, Gianni Muratore 95/1, Northants Photo 110/1, Paul Panayiotou 72/17, Edward Parker 79/36, PCL 100/7, 110/14, David Pearson 81/5, Photofusion Picture Library 44/5, 54/3, Photostock – Josef Mullek 84/9, Paul Prescott 25/1, Gary Roebuck 110/2, Daniel Rooney 110/11, Peter Scholes 22/9, Alex Segre 22/10, 26/5, 62/1, 121/4, Niel Setchfield 110/10, Shout 26/6, 146/8, Ian Simpson 85/21, Steve Skjold 56/33, Jack Sullivan 54/4, 58/7, 85/20, Tetra Images 23/17, The Photolibrary Wales 67/9, Peter Titmuss 24/11, 100/11, Arthur Turner 6/24, Colin Underhill 85/19, Francis Vachon 39/31, Vario Images GmbH & Co KG 23/18, 77/20, Ivan Vdovin 71/24, Lisa F Young 26/4

Art Directors and TRIP Photo Library: Juliet Highet 49/8, Helene Rogers 85/22, 120/2, 120/13

Trevor Clifford: 43/25, 46/1, 46/2, 46/4, 46/5, 46/6, 46/9, 46/15, 46/16, 46/17, 46/18, 47/1, 47/2, 47/3, 47/4, 47/5, 47/6, 47/7l, 47/8, 47/9, 47/17, 47/18, 47/20, 47/21, 47/22, 47/23, 47/24, 47/26, 47/27, 48/1, 48/3, 48/5, 48/7, 48/10, 48/11, 48/12, 48/13, 48/22, 48/27, 48/29, 49/1, 49/2, 49/3, 49/4, 49/5, 49/6, 49/7, 62/7, 62/16-19, 62/26, 63/1-10, 63/12-21, 63/30-34, 64/22-24, 67/3, 79/34, 82/1-10, 82/16, 82/24, 82/26, 85/24, 123/1

Corbis: 110/4

DK Cartography: 114-115, 116

DK Images: 120/1, 122/18, Victor Borg 110/5, Geoff Brightling 95/11, Andy Crawford 58/10, Steve Gorton 16/10, Sian Irvine 69/16, Howard Shooter 21/1, Lindsay Stock 120/12, Chris Stowers 26/1, Clive Streeter 27/32

Getty Images: 24/14, 26/19, 100/5, 100/10, 146/9, AFP 100/12, 109/8, Christopher Bissell 23/3, Peter Dazeley 24/7, 146/4, Tim Graham 100/3, David Oliver 23/12, Herman du Plessis 49/12, Visual Cuisines 65/23

iStockphoto: 122/3, Akarelias 23/19, Alina555 43/20, Gary Alvis 46/19, Andres Balcazar 44/16, Adrian Beesley 55/11, Black Jake 26/16, Daniel Cooper 27/30, Corstiaan Elzelingen, van 84/17,

dibrova 79/37, esp-imaging 110/7, Rafal Glebowski 123/6, Kharas 110/9, Leontura 52/29, Sean Locke 43/15, NoDerog 46/13, Franz Pfluegl 122/8, pixhook 46/14, Plainview 123/19, Pushlama 109/12, Francesca Rizzo 47/7r, Julian Rovagnati 56/30, Jo Ann Snover 46/12, Kais Tolmats 46/11, Marek Walica 47/7b, xyno 55/7, Yin Yang 49/14

Pearson Education Ltd: 70/23, 84/5, Arnos Design 62/4, Gareth Boden 39/3, 39/15b, 39/15t, Corbis 44/11, Image Source 100/2, istockphoto 48/14, 65/5, Mind Studio 21/20, Peter Morris 84/16, Photodisc 26/7, 43/9, 43/11, Photodisc / John Wang 100/6, Photodisc / Life File / Andrew War 100/8, Photodisc / Life File / Michael Evans 23/20, 146/2, Photodisc / Squared Studios 60/17, Jules Selmes 67/12r, 71/25, Devon Obugenga Shaw 25/11, Studio 8 / Clark Wiseman 82/30, 83/14, Ian Wedgewood 57/10

Photolibrary.com: age fotostock 122/12, Asia Images 28/11, Blend Images 23/5, 28/13, Corbis 45/24, Corbis / Zefa 6/23r, Creatas 49/13, Image Source 25/15, 146/7, image100 49/16, Monkey Business Images Ltd 56/11, 57/11, Zen Shui 28/14, View Stock 109/2, Warwick Kent 23/21

Press Association Images: PA Wire 100/4

PunchStock: Digital Vision 26/9

Rex Features: Action Press 110/8, Ilpo Musto 84/13, John Powell 84/2

Images reproduced with kind permission of Royal Mail Group Ltd: 82/22

Shutterstock: 43/18, Aznym Adam 61/34l, Andresr 41/3, 43/16, Robert Anthony 67/32, Yuri Arcurs 47/10, Teresa Azevedo 61/34r, Simone van den Berg 43/14, Orhan Cam 55/5, Paul Cowan 65/21, Michele Cozzolino 70/27, Danicek 66/2, David Davis 49/11, dundanim 84/12, Christopher Elwell 70/22, Fine Shine 122/16t, BW Folsom 52/24, Gago 45/9, Vladislav Gajic 55/14, gemphotography 84/6, Sandra Gligorijasevic 21/4, Golden Pixels LLC 6/28, Joe Gough 65/15, 65/24, 70/18, 70/24, 70/28, Iwona Grodzka 70/16, Hitdelight 53/7, Hau Hoang 53/13, Oliver Hoffmann 67/33, immanuel001 65/12, Infomages 60/2, Kadroff 47/14, Karkas 47/15, 48/9, 53/6, Robert Kneschke 58/22, knotsmaster 56/31, Sergey Lavrentev 55/12, Michael Ledray 44/7, Jin Young Lee 84/8, Teresa Levite 69/25, Emil Vasilev Lliev 70/25, Jim Lopes 43/8, luchschen 66/14, Masterpiece 123/5, MAT 36/14, Monkey Business Images 28/2, 62/9, Brett Mulcahy 65/29, NatUlrich 59/34, 149/2, nicobatista 122/16b, Zsolt Nyulaszi 43/12, Sas Partout 45/8, Losevsky Pavel 84/11, Vladislav Pavlovich 45/26, Photosani 122/17, picturepartners 60/10, Maureen Plainfield

93/11, Alexander Raths 44/8, Radu Razvan 53/23, riccar 123/8, Julián Rovagnati 122/1, Elzbieta Sekowska 65/28, Jane September 55/2, SerrNovik 55/8, Andrea Skjold 65/22, James Steidl 49/15, studiogi 66/3, Supertrooper 122/14, T-Design 41/1, Taratorki 65/19, Graca Victoria 65/25, vilax 122/19, Yegorius 84/19, Lisa F Young 23/10, 146/1

Thinkstock: 49/9, 56/34, Ablestock.com 23/14, 66/15, 146/3, Bananastock 99/6, 118/10, Michael Blann 39/1, 84/10, Brand X Pictures 23/8, 26/2, 60/20, Comstock 6/33, 21/16, 21/21, 22/2, 24/6, 24/15, 26/13, 28/9, 84/4, 106/15, 109/4, Creatas 23/13, 24/8, 45/1, 84/1, Digital Vision 23/1, 23/2, 26/14, 91/1, 97/6, George Doyle 39/10, 39/13, Goodshot 23/11, Hemera 43/1, 48/18, 53/8, 53/9, 53/11, 60/1, 60/3, 60/12, 61/33t, 61/35, 65/6, 65/16, 66/10, 67/1, 67/18, 70/21, 95/13, 123/22, 123/23, 153/7, iStockphoto 23/7, 25/2, 25/5, 26/8, 26/10, 27/33, 39/14, 44/1, 44/12, 46/3, catman73 47/16, 52/19, 59/31l, 59/31r, 60/4, 60/5, 60/6, 60/7, 60/8, 60/11, 60/13, 60/14, 60/15, 60/16, 60/18, 60/19, 61/8, 61/33b, 61/36, 63/35, 65/7, 65/9, 65/10, 65/11, 65/13, 65/14, 65/18, 65/20, 66/1, 66/7, 66/8, 66/9, 66/11, 66/12, 66/13, 66/16, 67/2, 67/12l, 67/13, 67/19, 67/30, 67/31, 67/34, 67/35, 67/36, 67/37, 70/26, 70/29, 70/30, 80/18, 80/21, 80/22, 85/16, 95/12, 97/12, 100/1, 100/9, 105/23, 110/12, 120/10, 122/2, 122/10, 122/15, 123/7, 123/9, 123/17, 123/18, 123/25, 149/4, 149/6, 149/7, 153/1, Jetta Productions 54/6, 56/32, Jupiterimages 30/11, 39/5, 39/16, 43/3, 43/7, 43/10, 44/19, 84/3, Lifesize 21/18, 23/16, 25/8, Photodisc 109/14, PhotoObjects.net 27/31, 37/4, 37/10, Photos.com 86/28, Pixland 25/3, 25/19, Polka Dot 21/17, 23/9, 25/4, 25/6, 25/17, 80/17, 97/9, 146/6, RL Productions 84/18, Stockbyte 22/1, 25/14, 25/16, 26/15, 28/1, 146/10, svry 65/17, James Woodson 54/5

Cover images *Front:* **Pearson Education Ltd:** Photodisc, Tudor Photography; **Thinkstock:** Comstock, iStockphoto, Photodisc, Photos.com, Stockbyte; *Back:* **Thinkstock:** iStockphoto, Photodisc, Stockbyte

AUDIO CDs TRACK LIST

CD 1

PEOPLE

2	Personal data	1'49
3	The family	0'59
4	Daily routine / home activities	0'57

HOUSING

5	Places to live: flat and house	1'10
6	The kitchen	1'07
7	Kitchen equipment	1'29
8	The bathroom	1'23
9	The bedroom	1'06
10	The living room	1'05
11	The dining room	1'18
12	The nursery and baby accessories	1'04
13	The utility room	1'01
14	The garden	1'19
15	Gardening	1'22
16	Floor plan of a house	1'16

WORK / OCCUPATIONS

17	At home / housework	1'08
18	Getting a job	0'34
19	Jobs 1	0'59
20	Jobs 2	0'46
21	Jobs 3	1'07
22	Jobs 4	1'10
23	The office	1'39
24	Office activities	0'53
25	In a workshop	1'35
26	In a factory	0'54
27	On a construction site	1'12
28	In a hotel	1'02
29	Dealing with crime	0'49

THE BODY

30	Parts of the body 1	1'36
31	Parts of the body 2	1'24
32	Physical descriptions	1'24
33	Verbs of action 1	1'00
34	Verbs of action 2	0'52
35	At the hairdresser's and the beauty salon	1'45
36	Hairstyling, make-up and manicure	1'33

HEALTH

37	Minor ailments	1'14
38	Medicine: at the chemist's	1'06
39	Medical care	1'19
40	At the hospital	1'16
41	Dental and eye care	1'30

CLOTHES AND FASHION

42	Men's and women's wear 1	1'11
43	Men's and women's wear 2	1'35
44	Men's and women's wear 3	1'41
45	Men's and women's wear 4	1'02
46	Describing clothes	1'09
47	Colours and patterns	1'08
48	Fabrics, sewing and knitting	1'33
49	Accessories and jewellery	1'55

CD 2

SCHOOL

1	Education in Great Britain	0'32
2	Playground and pre-school	1'16
3	The school	1'46
4	School subjects	1'15
5	College, adult education, library	1'23

FOOD

6	Vegetables 1	1'44
7	Vegetables 2	1'10
8	Fruit	2'15
9	At the supermarket 1	1'36
10	At the supermarket 2	1'46
11	Supermarket counters	1'50
12	At the restaurant 1	1'43
13	At the restaurant 2	1'22
14	Fast food and snacks	1'56
15	Containers and quantities	1'39
16	Cooking	1'34
17	Breakfast, lunch, dinner	1'40

TRANSPORT

18	Public transport	1'26
19	Private transport 1	1'35
20	Private transport 2	2'17
21	Road and road signs	1'30
22	Road and road signs	1'16
23	At the airport 1	1'31
24	At the airport 2	1'45
25	Water transport	1'31

COMMUNITY

26	Money	2'53
27	The city / city life 1	1'27
28	The city / city life 2	1'01
29	At the post office	1'53
30	At the newsagent's	1'48
31	At the shopping mall	1'10
32	Emergencies	1'49

SPORTS

33	Team and spectator sports 1	2'18
34	Team and spectator sports 2	1'04
35	Individual sports 1	1'33
36	Individual sports 2	2'10
37	Water sports	2'10
38	Winter sports	1'17
39	At the gym	1'23

RECREATION

40	Entertainment	1'22
41	Hobbies and games 1	1'39
42	Hobbies and games 2	0'50
43	Musical instruments	1'45
44	At the beach	1'27
45	In the country	1'25
46	Places to visit 1	1'14
47	Places to visit 2	0'59

CD 3

ANIMALS

1	Pets	1'08
2	Farm animals	1'12
3	Wild animals	1'58
4	Fish and sea animals	1'29
5	Birds	1'37
6	Insects and small animals	1'28

NUMBERS, HOLIDAYS, MAPS

7	Numbers	3'00
8	Shapes	1'49
9	Calendar, festivals and religions 1	1'52
10	Calendar, festivals and religions 2	0'52
11	Time	2'23
12	The UK and the Republic of Ireland	0'31
13	The United States	0'35
14	The World	0'22
15	Europe	1'00

THE ENVIRONMENT

16	Landscape features	1'53
17	Seasons and weather	1'37
18	Space	1'41

COMPUTERS, HOME AND OFFICE ELECTRONICS

19	Computers and software	1'59
20	The Internet	1'03
21	Home electronics and telecommunications 1	1'22
22	Home electronics and telecommunications 2	1'38

EXPRESSING ONESELF

23	Adjectives 1	0'54
24	Adjectives 2	1'43
25	Prepositions 1	0'50
26	Prepositions 2	1'07